A Heart for Truth

A Heart for Truth
Taking Your Faith to College

Greg Spencer

BAKER BOOK HOUSE
Grand Rapids, Michigan 49516

Copyright 1992 by
Baker Book House Company
P. O. Box 6287
Grand Rapids, MI 49516-6287

ISBN: 0-8010-8331-1

Printed in the United States of America

Scripture quotations are from the New International Version. Copyright 1973, 1978, 1984 International Bible Society. Used by permission of Zondervan Bible Publishers.

Cartoons by David Slonim

For **Janet,**
who made this *Heart*
and my heart gentler

Contents

Acknowledgments   9
Introduction: On Leaving Home   11

**Part
One: You <u>Can</u> Take It with You**

   1   The Answer: "Go to College, of
      Course"   19
   2   Education: The Good, the Bad, and the
      Ugly   27
   3   Gearing Up for Culture Shock   39
   4   Faith and Morality 101   55

**Part
Two: The Angelic Beast in the Mirror**

   5   My Basic Problem Is That I Take
      Me Wherever I Go   67
   6   Putting the Good News First   77
   7   Can I Love Me If I Know Me?   89

**Part
Three: Those Whom We Love**

   8   Friendship in an Age of Kleenex   101
   9   Sex: It's Both Less and More
      Than You Think   115
  10   Is Dating Emotional Fornication?   135

**Part
Four: The Intellectual(!) Christian**

11 What? I'm Also Expected to Think?   155
12 Enemies of the Thinking Christian   171
13 Not to Worry: The God of Creation Is Also
   Lord over Karl Marx's World   189
14 Seeing a Penny and Hearing a Bell   205

**Two
Postscripts**

Writing for Dr. Pagan   213
Field-Tested, Sensory-Satisfying Study
Habits Guide   221

Recommended Reading   229

Acknowledgments

In somewhat chronological order, praises go to Dominic LaRusso for pointing toward the truth, to the McKenzie Study Center for providing the freedom to begin, to Westmont colleagues David Downing, Paul Willis, Randy Vandermey, and Lisa Studley for their encouragement and wise critique, and to Laura Wilson for her editor's eye and Olympian stamina. Great relief came in the form of a Westmont Faculty Development Grant and through Dan Van't Kerkhoff's patience.

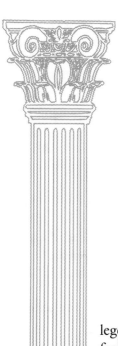

Introduction
On Leaving Home

> What could be more delightful than
> to have in the same few minutes all
> the fascinating terrors of going abroad
> combined with all the humane secu-
> rity of coming home again?
>
> G. K. Chesterton

When the time came to put my col-
lege-bound suitcases in the car, the familiar
faces of family, friends, and Biff (the wiener
dog) all sobbed an earnest farewell, except
my sister who was glad to get the whole
house to herself. I kissed them all (especially Biff), boarded my friend Nina's Pinto,
said goodbye to Santa Maria, and set sail
for San Salvador. Well, not exactly, but
Columbus and I did have a number of
things in common. We both were intrepid
explorers, brave and daring, who would

11

chart unknown territory and come back to tell about it. He, with the blessing of Spain, discovered America. I, with a contract in blood to write my parents weekly, brought my ship to port at the Dorm of No Return. Actually, I couldn't wait to leave home. No more high school cliques. No more John O'Connor's rude face. No more having to be in by the Magic Hour or risk becoming a pumpkin for a week. No more teacher's dirty looks. But you can't have everything, so going away to school also had all of the less-appealing ingredients of any great adventure: danger, risk, anxiety.

Come to think of it, why was I looking forward to leaving home? So many bad things could happen. What if I don't fit in? What if my roommate is impossible to live with? What if I can't make good grades? What if the people I want to get to know have drug-glazed eyes every Friday? What if Jesus seems as distant as the answer to that first essay question in World Civilization?

College turned out to be all the adventure I could have asked for. I loved the freedom but hated the lack of direction. I enjoyed making new friends but disliked the lonely evenings without my old buddies. I was intellectually stimulated in the classroom but received my first "D." I was thrilled to share my faith with friends but was quite embarrassed when I tried to point out the "errors of evolution" to a biology major.

Indeed, leaving home for college is an exploration in many ways. Trouble is, though we might put our name on the map, we might just as easily get lost or be eaten by the natives. What we really want, as G. K. Chesterton writes, is to have an expedition that contains the qualities of both wonder and welcome. The best sort of adventure is one in which we have all the fun of discovering some new place "without the disgusting necessity of landing there." This sense of "practical romance," as he calls it, this combination of something strange and something secure, is not only a fundamental

human need, but an insightful way to think about your collegiate experience.

Though you must land and make your way through the jungle of academia, you will complete your expedition in better shape if you find paths that are trustworthy and yet afford excellent views. My hope is that this book will help you find a few of those paths so you can avoid needless and risky trailblazing. Along the way, as you learn how to take your faith to college, you will probably find that the experience becomes increasingly wondrous and welcoming.

For college to be *wondrous,* you need to have a solid way to think about higher education. I call this perspective "a heart for truth." If you approach learning with an appreciation for all that God might have in store for you, you will develop a passion to know, a desire to "think God's thoughts after him." Among other things, this involves applying your faith to your studies, exploring the boundaries of what it means to believe, and trusting in the Lordship of Christ.

For college to be *welcoming,* you would do well to attend to the wisdom of the Scriptures as they address issues that usually confront students. As your world expands, you may find your place in it challenged, and so your concerns over "self" and "identity" need to be addressed. As your immediate environment changes, especially your circle of friends and romantic interests, your views about relationships will be put to the test. As you grow in your application of the good mind you have been given, a number of challenges for the college-student-as-thinker will become important, including dealing with doubt and cynicism. These are the kinds of issues that will be addressed in the chapters ahead: education, identity, relationships, thinking, and studies. As you read, feel free to take any direction that would most meet your needs of the moment. In other words, any chapter works on its own as well as in the order presented.

Wherever you begin or finish, my hope is that you will end up with a greater trust in Jesus Christ, who in his own way was a kind of Adventurer, too. We sometimes forget that he left his secure and joyful home, his Father's house, and went to live for a time among rather difficult (if not beastly) people. And though he was welcomed by only a few, he brought his own kind of wonder, by turning water into wine, healing skin diseases and sin diseases, feeding whomever he wished, and bringing clear, true hope into the world.

As you struggle with the temptations and uncertainties of college life, look for comfort and help from the One who braved even stranger territory. Though he died on his journey (and you may have some "dying" of sorts ahead, too), he rose victorious and returned home. If you follow him, even as he followed the Father, the faith that you take to college will become the mature, robust belief of the experienced Christian adventurer.

What's in Your Heart?

1. What would the ideal college experience be like? Is your ideal likely to occur?
2. What do you most hope will happen in college? What are your greatest fears?
3. In what ways would you describe your educational experience so far as "wondrous" or "welcoming"?

Part One
You <u>Can</u> Take It with You

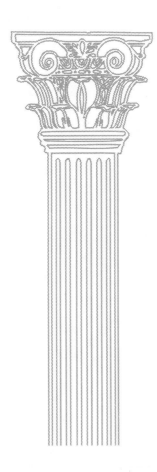

The Answer: "Go to College, of Course"

Better to ask twice than lose your way once.

Danish proverb

I remember well the springtime of my senior year in high school. The sense of relief, of liberty, of triumph. The excitement of entering into a new phase of my life. Could my world do anything but get better? What would the future hold? Fame? Romance? Success? And how about after Grad Night?

I can tell you exactly what happened *after* Grad Night. Everyone from the dentist to the dormouse asked THE QUESTION: "What are you gonna do after graduation?" After my initial panic, I'd gather my wits and reply coolly, "Go to college, of course."

19

Beneath my suave facade, I didn't have much of an idea of what I really wanted to do about my future. And, if pressed, I would have had a difficult time justifying my decision to continue in school. However, since no one ever asked *why* I was going to college, I never needed to justify my decision. Everybody ought to go to college, right?

While this seems to be true, "everybody ought to" has been wrong before. Many cute little cliff-leaping lemmings have been known to follow the crowd, only to find themselves thirty stories up without a parachute. "I was just following the tail in front of me" will not be a very persuasive argument halfway down. Although lemmings tend to ignore look-before-you-leap advice, any prospective or current college student would do well to ask a few questions. What are some possible motivations for going to college? Do you have some sense that your purposes and the college's purposes mesh? The following open-book test might be helpful. It will not be graded. At least not by me.

In the list below, what is the principal reason
you are going to college?

1. to meet new people
2. to reach my potential
3. to learn to be on my own
4. to make lots of money
5. to be trained for a job
6. to get away from home
7. because all my friends are going
8. to find a spouse
9. because my parents want me to
10. Some or all of the above

As with any good review of an exam, the possible answers will be examined one by one. First, "to meet new people." Certainly, some of the "newest" people can be

found in college. Some of your acquaintances will become instant friends and others may develop more slowly into friendships that last a lifetime. Of course, you will meet many a forgettable character in college as well. The curious thing, though, is that while college *is* a good place to meet people and have stimulating conversations, you do not need to go to college for that. The same goal could be met by going to an aerobics class or joining the Committee to Select an Official National Insect. So college is hardly unique in this area.

If going to college to meet people is not the perfect motive, how about number two, "to reach my potential"? That all depends on what you mean by this. College *can* tap and fulfill certain kinds of potential, but your attitudes and choices about college life dramatically influence this process. If a stretching experience is all you desire, a wilderness trek or starting a new business might be in order. College is not the only potential-tapping option available. You could hitchhike around Europe, work at sculpture, or go on a missions trip to Panama. College *may* tap into new reserves of skill and strengths better than other places. But why?

"To learn to be on my own" is choice number three. Although independence is a natural and acceptable ambition, might not this motive be frustrated by the demands of your studies? If you were to move out of the house and get a job, you could be a budding individualist without interference from nasty professors and annoying exams. Living on a budget will stimulate independence faster than your parents can say "a two-hundred-dollar phone bill!" You can learn to be on your own as easily outside of college as inside it. Then again, college can significantly influence the growing independent person that you're becoming. How? What does college offer that other experiences lack?

Numbers four and five have in common an economic theme: "to make lots of money" and "to be trained for a job." Increasingly, students have some specific vocational pursuit in mind as they enter college. Since college graduates, on average, make more money than their less-degreed counterparts, a financial orientation might seem to be warranted. However, although a college degree will probably get you a job that will keep you *out* of the rain, it will not necessarily provide you with a better roof than those who work *in* the rain. You may not make more or be happier than the carpenter down the street. But even if you did, a single-minded monetary goal may not be the best motive for going to college. You will miss something if you evaluate every collegiate decision for its potential financial gain. Still, is it wrong to think of the future and desire to support yourself and a family? How can college affect your approach to money-making?

We come now to the major reason for my own entry into the Halls of Academe: choice number six—"to get away from home." I simply couldn't bear the thought of staying in town any longer. The people from whom I most wanted to distance myself were staying in town. My parents were staying in town. The tough guys were staying in town. And so was beautiful Carrie Weston, who at one point thought I was a grand vision of masculinity, but by graduation thought I looked like a petrified wart. One might well ask, if all I needed was to "get away," why didn't I just leave for destinations unknown? To my way of thinking at the time, that answer was too simple. I needed not only to get "out" but to get "in"—that is, to find a place where I belonged, inhabited by peers who were more like me. Besides, what would I do in another town? Get a full-time job? Get serious. Maybe college was the answer, as it seemed to be for most of my friends.

So, option seven beckons: "because all my friends are going." Whether we admit it or not, peer pressure squeezes us very tightly. What if everyone else went to school and you stayed home? The mere sight of those status-shouting college decals would stab you every time. Imagine the shame of a blank sweatshirt. Who wants to be a nobody? Who wants to be left out? Who wants to be thought of as a loser who couldn't get in?

Should you go to college for a decal? Hardly—maybe there's something worth examining here. As a motive, this option accepts the logic of "taking the next step." Just as high school was the next step after junior high, so college seems to be the most natural thing to do after high school. This has not always been the case. In the early 1900s, for example, most people were finished with their education by the eighth grade. By 1935, completing high school was a commendable achievement. Now, the norm is for most to begin at least the bachelor's degree, and the next generation will probably be expected to plod on into graduate school. Perhaps those in the twenty-first century will never be allowed out! A worthy question for the next-steppers is: "College is the next step to *what?*" Ordinary maturity? Trivial pursuit? Spouse hunting? What are you "stepping" toward? Will the decal help here? What is the decal supposed to represent?

Whereas the goals reviewed above do provide some strong arguments, answer eight is transparently weak. The best one could say about "to find a spouse" is that it is an honest answer. Although it may be among your reasons for attending college, surely this alone is not a good reason for filling a seat in a classroom and paying off student loans for twenty years. If this were a worthy main motivation for attending college, I suppose the best scenario would be for like-minded men and women to find each other as freshmen so they can drop out, get married, and save all that tuition money.

Parental pressure—number nine—is a trickier proposition. "Because my parents want me to" may contain more validity than it seems at first glance. Sometimes parents indeed know best and recognize that their Sleeping Prince or Princess will more likely awaken in a collegiate environment. Many students who are resentful of parental pressure at eighteen are grateful at twenty-two. However, sometimes it is the parents who need the waking up. Parents who send their children to college simply to get them out of the house or to brag about their collegiate status or to protect them from the Big Bad World do not necessarily have their children's best interests at heart. At any rate, one could ask again, "Why college?"

Taken together or separately, these nine possibilities cover at least some of the motives that might ricochet around in your mind as people shoot off the question "Why college?" As important and legitimate as these concerns are, none of them taps into the one unique contribution that college offers. At some point, if you are not merely to go through the motions, you must match your motivation with the purposes of undergraduate institutions. What is unique about college? What could possibly have been omitted in the list just examined? Brace yourself. Cleverly disguised as impractical discussions and boring busy-work, all these years a dark, hidden agenda has been inflicted upon you by devious and conspiratorial adult authority figures: *education.*

Contrary to some preconceptions, the *one* advantage that college has over moving into an apartment, going on a death-wish wilderness trek, or undertaking any other experience after high school is premeditated, instructed learning. The importance of this difference is that unless education is a *primary* motive (not necessarily the only one), college may be a frustrating and disappointing four years. It will certainly be less than what it could be. If you think of education as something to get out of the way so that you can chase the goals you really have for the collegiate experience, much of what college has to offer will be missed, resisted, or rejected. College is an expensive place to do what most of us little larvae will do anyway—mature beyond the caterpillar stage.

I am not condemning the other reasons for attending a college or university (I had some of them myself), nor am I suggesting that many ought not even apply (some students dramatically improve their performance with the least attractive motives). Instead, a simple rule should be considered: When expectations correspond to reality, satisfaction more likely follows. Besides, if you want to benefit from your college experience, shouldn't you position yourself to receive what college is best at delivering? There is more at stake than you may realize. College life may mean many different things, but when the educational component does not increase in importance, all the rest tends to become less meaningful.

Many students will change from caterpillar to butterfly at college. The point is that knowing how to take advantage of the quality of these cocoon years will affect the shape and brightness of your future wings. If, after four years, you just turn into a dull-colored moth, Mom and Pop may think they wasted a whole lot of nectar.

What's in Your Heart?

1. Answer this question: "Why are you going to college?" Survey a few friends for their responses. Do you resonate with any of the reasons provided?
2. If college life consisted only of the classroom experience, what would your attitude toward it be?
3. Describe your most encouraging and most discouraging educational experiences.

Education:
The Good, the Bad, and the Ugly

I can point the finger but I cannot supply the vision.

St. Augustine

Let's suppose that you are leaning toward the conclusions of the previous chapter. Although you wrestle with your share of motivational monsters, you are ready to state categorically that "to get an education" will be your top priority for at least four years. Feels great just to say it, right? Now, before you get carried away into academic euphoria, you might like to think about two related questions: What is education anyway? What is an appropriate attitude toward education? (And when will this guy stop asking annoying questions?) My point is that you can make a commitment to "education" yet not have a concrete idea about what education means, much less its purpose.

A friend of mine who is a philosopher once said that when it comes to education, "Everyone is either a philosopher or a drug addict." He was suggesting that there are two fundamentally opposed visions of education. Students are motivated by either a love for truth (the philosopher) or a love for comfort (the drug addict). Students may not literally either debate Hegel or snort cocaine, but they tend to strive either to discover what is real at any cost or to avoid the uncomfortable parts of reality at any cost. In this sense I have been both philosopher and drug addict.

During my senior year in high school, I dated a girl off and on for several months (mainly off). Jean was a cute, bubbly blond who smiled adoringly at me. Naive soul that I was, I fell for those blinking blue eyes. After I committed my enduring like to her and she to me, I did what was only natural: I broke up with her. About a week later, I decided that I couldn't live without her, not for a single second (or at least for this particular Saturday night), so we made up and made out. During the next week, at some inopportune moment, I told Jean that I never wanted to see her again. As if this wasn't enough to win the Slimiest Scum of the Sewer Award, I did this two more times. Why? Because I was a drug addict. At seventeen I would overindulge in any number of things that would make me feel good. I wasn't foolish enough to shoot up heroin or take LSD, but I was reckless enough to sacrifice mental, spiritual, moral, and financial health for the drugs of popularity and romance.

"Drug addicts" are comfort-seekers who are more concerned with anesthetizing their lives against unpleasantness than enduring any painful truth. In my situation, I preferred the comfortable status of having a pretty girlfriend to the truth that my commitment lacked integrity. A philosopher would have chosen the truth over a lie. I could have exercised this virtue by resisting the allures of a friendly female whom I knew deep-down I did not care for.

Education and romance can both be divided along these lines. Just as there are many reasons to go to college, one of which is to get an education, there are many reasons to get an education, one of which is to follow the vision of the philosopher. To be a "philosopher" you need not think in brainy, abstract terms about everything. *(As the bus came into view, the philosopher cocked his head strangely to the right and with a glazed look in his eyes said, "Why a bus?")* You don't even need to major in philosophy. What you do need is a clear perspective about truth and a certain passion for getting it.

Two "Drug Addict" Views of Education

A Ticket to a Job

Some students—that is to say comfort addicts who disguise themselves as students—are only concerned with gaining entry to the Real World. In this fantasy (hallucination?), these students walk through the graduation line and pick up a diploma, which is shaped like a huge movie ticket. Instead of saying "Bachelor of Arts," the ticket reads "Admit One to Career Excitement, Financial Reward, and Real World Action." Ticket paid for, these students go looking for the nearest usher, what they call an employer, so they can make some use of the ticket. Maybe they'll even keep the stub.

Students with this attitude see their education as only a means to an end, an end dominated by a lifestyle of prestige and financial success. If that weren't a limited enough view of existence, what about the value of the ticket itself? A ticket is only worth whatever you can get for it. Once used, the ticket is either discarded or kept for sentimental value. In their preoccupation with future comfort, these students regularly dismiss anything that might deter them from that end and value their education only insofar as they can relate it to an identifiable career option. Their favorite question is "What good will this do me when I graduate?" They don't want to hear about some impractical requirement that cannot be explained in terms of job training. The diploma may go on the wall, but the college degree *as education* doesn't seem to matter.

The diploma-as-ticket students are not to be criticized for desiring something practical out of their college years or for considering their ultimate livelihood. The problem is that they are so preoccupied with the future that they miss what could be gained in the nonfinancially-rewarding present. As the saying goes, "If you think too much about where you're going, you lose respect for where you are."

In addition, I suspect that there are problems in these students' view of what they call the Real World. Just as a drug alters an addict's perception of his or her surroundings, sometimes providing the user with too much confidence, this view of the Real World tends to be rather dreamy. Those who are so anxious to "get out of school" often wonder later what the rush was all about. I have received many letters from graduates who complain that they feel restricted by the very world they thought would free them. They soon discover that the treadmill of paying bills may be *real*, but it is not somehow "more Real" than college. It is not consistently more pleasant or more exciting. Suddenly, studying the great minds of the past and present looks pretty intriguing, at least as Real as selling widgets or getting up at 6:30 A.M. for a 45-minute commute. The simple truth is that life with a diploma in hand is often more stressful than the process of getting one. In fact, a recent Gallup survey reported that 85 percent of Americans do not look forward to their workday. So much for the Real World. A ticket does not always buy what we think it will. And what we want is sometimes less worth having than we realize.

A Series of Hoops to Jump Through

Others see education as an assembly line of knowledge where students travel on a conveyor belt, getting injected with 50cc of biology here and 75cc of literature there, and packaged for distribution. At the end of the line, the Quality Inspector stamps "Graduate" on their foreheads. Depending on the evaluation, the inspector can also designate "Prime," "Choice," or "Good." Students who take this view of college like to say that they "can't wait to get General Education courses out of the way" or that "Dr. Dull's course is the easiest way to meet the math requirement."

From this perspective, education is not so much a means to an end as it is an annoyance, an obstacle course, a game to be won by discovering subversive short cuts. The fun is in beating the system with the least amount of effort. The main problem with this view is that the pattern of seeking comfort at all costs soon becomes an addiction and "getting by" becomes the norm. The inherent joys of education are lost, as is the possibility of fulfilling that wondrous potential spoken of earlier. Although these students may learn something in spite of themselves, they tend to see the whole process as a dreary paper chase through a series of meaningless and arbitrary hoops. It is hard to see value in things that we try to "get out of the way."

Having a Heart for Truth

In contrast to the limitations of the previous two views, "having a heart for the truth" sees education in far broader terms and embraces it as part of the life of faith. Instead of the addict's vision of education as a prerequisite for future pleasures or as a root canal that should be endured no longer than necessary, the philosopher's vision of education states that learning is good. In fact, when we search for wisdom, we love God with our minds.

I remember studying for a music-appreciation class one day when the thought struck me that every strand of knowledge is part of the larger fabric called truth. I had previously compartmentalized knowledge into neat categories such as drama, sociology, or physics. Suddenly, I saw that music, which seemed on the surface to be the least rational of all the arts, was also a mathematical science, with measured notes and numerical directions. Disciplines as varied as biology and accounting seemed to coalesce into a seamless cloth, an unbroken tapestry that had its source in God himself.

My specific conclusion doesn't really matter. What is important is that I had an "Aha!" moment, an intellectual breakthrough that gave me a sense of the texture of truth. My cold mind had been warmed by this insight, and my passion grew to see more and more of the fabric of God's world. I think I see it now as a woven carpet under my feet, which holds me up and eases my journey, and as a protective tent, which shelters me from the untruths that assail us like so much acid rain.

"A heart for truth" is a passionate desire to know whatever God would have us know. It is an acknowledgment that we have been given a wonderful gift, the mind, and a greater gift, the liberty to care for it—to nurture it after God's own thoughts. That God, by his grace, has enabled us to perceive the truth at all is a glorious thing, and we have the responsibility to become stewards of our intelligence.

To have a heart for truth is to fulfill Jesus' command to love God with our heart, soul, *mind,* and strength (Mark 12:30). When we learn anything, from the ordinary to the profound, we can bless our Creator, the fount of all that is. Our appreciation is a way of loving him. So, too, is our pursuit of the truth. It is a way of saying, "What you have made is worthy of study, worthy of knowing." Think of it this way: If you had a dear friend who was a painter, part of loving that person would be to say, "Oh, please, may I see all your work? What you've done is so beautiful." And so we inquire of the heavenly Artist.

This "truth" that is our passion is not restricted to, strictly speaking, theological concepts or religious experiences. Bark-eating beetles, Pascal's conic formulae, Duke Ellington's jazz, Monet's painting, and Plato's dialogues may all be studied as enthusiastically as John Milton's devotional poetry or Martin Luther's Ninety-five Theses. Another way to put it is that in some way *everything* is "theological" in that everything is part of the world God made and loves. Perhaps the most important quality of those who possess a *heart* for truth is that they do not have only a *head* for truth. They realize that "head knowledge" may be only memorized facts, details that can be learned and quickly forgotten as part of a hoop-jumping mentality. Some students seem to think that the brain can hold only so much information. They hope that the answers they write on an exam will flow from the brain down their arm, into the pen, and onto the paper, never to take up space in the brain again. A *heart* for truth goes deeper. It is motivated by the desire to learn fully, even fervently, and to integrate any new knowledge ultimately into "wisdom." The search for truth is not satisfied until head meets heart such that knowledge is applied and genuinely expressed in the mind, body, and soul. For example, those with a heart for truth recognize that the Good Life is not so much "looking beautiful and having things" as it is "having beauty of soul and looking for the truth in things." Those who follow this vision not only intellectually agree with this version of the good life but try to live out its principles as fully as possible, even if it means being unlike their peers. They would prefer to be uncomfortably nonconformist and "in the truth" than pleasantly conformist and living a lie. Does this make them self-righteous snobs? No, for that would not be in keeping with the truth which speaks of our need to be humble before heaven.

One could say that without applied knowledge, true learning has not taken place. Social critic Malcolm Muggeridge has said that in modern education the professor's notes become the student's notes without going through the minds of either. Too often true! But the heart for truth disdains this kind of learning and is not content with mere repetition. It is one thing to list ten types of nonpoisonous mushrooms on an exam. It is another thing to trust that knowledge by picking a wild mushroom and eating it. Serious consequences are certainly no less true in the moral realm.

Another way to capture this vision of learning is to think of five levels of education: awareness, familiarity, knowledge, understanding, and wisdom. Often, when we say we "know" something, the life of David, for example, we may only be "familiar" with it, some of us only "aware." Likewise, although we may be able to recite David's biography, personality, and related biblical references—and possess "understanding" to the degree that we can put the ideas into our own words—we may not have integrated into "wisdom" the full picture of David's life.

When we turn our ear to wisdom and search for understanding as for hidden treasure (Prov. 2:2, 4), we value education. Why? Do we search because we *must*, because we fear a vengeful God who punishes slackers? No. God is not an angry professor who takes delight in the quantity of red marks he can scrawl across an exam. He wants us to know the truth more than we do, but in his mercy never gives us more than we can bear.

Through this approach to learning, you can view your college studies within the domain of your life in the kingdom of God. Since the hard work of studying is part of what it means to have a heart for truth, you will find no more success when you pray your way through British Poetry 202 than when you lay hands on a defunct engine. God does not seem to have set up certain "spiritual" activities to circumvent "physical" activities. Life is not meant to be so easily split into these neat compartments. For example, I am not necessarily *more* spiritual if I neglect my studies so that I can outline the Book of Romans or coordinate a ministry team. Instead, if my calling is to be a student, then whenever I study I am involved in a spiritual task. Just as a heart for truth sees knowledge as a seamless fabric, so it sees the life of the spiritual person as part of the tapestry, wherever his or her thread is connected to the overall pattern.

Sometimes we are awakened to this idea when we least expect it. For an English class, I was required to read the short story "A Good Man Is Hard to Find." In it, one of Flannery O'Connor's rough characters says of the grandmother, "She would of been a good woman, if it [sic] had been somebody there to shoot her every minute of her life[sic]." I remember being stunned by the power of those words, so shocking in the context. But the second shock was this: They were in one sense true! After I had identified with the grandmother because she talked about prayer, suddenly I saw her as a hypocrite, an empty husk, a shrill creature on the border of hell itself. As I finished the story, I realized that although I read it for my short-story course, there was more to it than that. I didn't read it for the grade or the professor's requirements. I read it for the truth that was in it. I read it for what it had to say to me about shallow appearances. But—more importantly—*I read it unto God.* In that instant, I knew that I had an answer to "Why go to college?" I was going to learn; not to get a job or a diploma, not my professors' or my parents' approval, not even for my own good, but for the sake of God. I was learning to desire God with my mind. In so doing, I would love him, show that I believed in him, and obey him. Loving God with the mind is not only a pleasure; it is part of the greatest commandment that Jesus gave to us. We are privileged to be able to follow so high a calling.

Faith Is Not a Rabbit's Foot

To say that education can be conceived of as a heart for truth is also to say something about the nature of faith. Unlike some views of trusting God, this one contends that faith is not a unique part of the soul that is mysteriously isolated from the rest of life. Unfortunately, too many Christians carry around their faith like a good-luck charm or security blanket. Is it possible we are more than a little superstitious? Who can help us resolve this issue?

Good old Plato. Where would we be without his reminding us that the first point in any discussion is to define one's terms? "Education" needed definition, and that discussion led to an explanation of the main title of this book: *A Heart for Truth*. Now the idea of "faith" needs some explication if we are to come to terms with the subtitle: *Taking Your Faith to College*.

One image that comes to mind is of a guy getting ready to go out to meet the world on his own. As he heads for the door, he takes along a number of things without which he would feel unprepared. He grabs his wallet, keys, comb, checkbook, and, for good measure, a little rabbit's foot he's carried since second grade. For some strange reason, the rabbit's foot has usually given him a special feeling, an extra bit of hope that things will go his way.

Some people view "faith" in this way. They see faith as a magical insurance policy, a talisman they can grasp in a crisis, in order to stimulate a hopeful feeling. And the advantage of this faith-charm is that it can be kept in their pockets, hidden from sight until "good fortune" is needed. This is *not* what I mean by "taking your faith to college." Faith is not a rabbit's foot. If our faith is to be more than superstition, we cannot pick it up or leave it behind as we please.

Instead, faith in God is never static. It is a relational quality that is either growing or diminishing. Whether it is becoming more central to your identity or less central, a meaningful faith is not something that can be merely tacked on to the rest of your life. Unlike a rabbit's foot, faith has to do with more than those crisis moments when you need a little boost. Faith has to do with everything.

Faith in God is not unlike a child's trust in his or her parents. Children who believe in the goodness and wisdom of their parents will trust what their parents have said, even when the parents are not nearby. Children who "put on" trust in their parents when they are home, and "take off" trust when they are elsewhere, demonstrate that they do not really *believe* in their parents. If little Joanie at home said, "Of course, Mother dearest, I believe you when you say that playing with fire is dangerous," and then later set the school's library on fire, we might indeed question the sincerity of her faith!

So, too, taking your faith to college means neither leaving it at home nor putting it in your pocket. It is to integrate faith into your total experience. It is a recognition that you can trust God in everything, knowing that he will open the doors of your life to Jesus, including the doors marked "studies," "friends," or "career."

Faith in God provides so much more hope than a rabbit's foot stuffed into one's pocket. In the home called the soul, faith is the central feature of every room, not a special room off to the side called "the spiritual room." In the place where we live, faith may manifest itself as a bed for rest or a chair for study, a table around which companions laugh or a tree near which truthseekers argue. In short, faith in God is about life centered on him, a relationship and perspective that is meant to transform every aspect of our lives. As the nineteenth-century writer George MacDonald puts it:

> Be thou my home, my fire, my chamber blest,
> My book of wisdom, loved of all the best;
> Oh, be my friend, each day still newer found,
> As the eternal days and nights go round!

The truly faithful have a resolve to see God for who he is, the rightful King of all that is, from the mundane experiences of practical jokes in the dorm to the wonder of human blood cells. Taking your faith to college, then, is not picking up a rabbit's foot when you leave the house; it is inviting Jesus into every room and circumstance in which you live.

What's in Your Heart?

1. What does the quotation by Augustine—"I can point the finger but I cannot supply the vision"—have to

do with both parts of the title of this book? How does it specifically relate to this chapter?

2. In what ways have you been a "philosopher" or a "drug addict" in your attitude toward education? What moves you from one position to the other?

3. How would you respond to the three views of education discussed?

Gearing Up for Culture Shock

Part of me is over here and part of
me is over there!
  The Scarecrow of Oz

A few years ago my wife and I were
traveling across Europe for the summer.
Although we had a wonderful time traips-
ing from castle to cathedral, we had not
journeyed far before we noticed that things
were done a bit differently here and there.
Sometimes, the differences were quaint or
fascinating; other times, they made us feel
uneasy. For example, ice cubes were almost
impossible to find. Europeans seemed to
think that Cokes would keep cool in the
garage. Honestly. And (the nerve of those
foreigners) people spoke their own language in their own country! Since we
toured by car, we rarely met other Americans and were forced to rely on a puny

phrase book to make our way through strange subways and intimidating grocery stores.

One disturbing event occurred when we were celebrating our seventh wedding anniversary in a Paris restaurant. What could be better? How romantic. How chic. How expensive! After pitting our phrase book against the menu and coming up with such delicacies as "roast wrench," we took the waiter's recommendation and ordered *cervelle*. When our romantic, chic dinner arrived, we eagerly stared at the meat but saw only a maze of weird, squiggly lines.

"What in the world is that?" my wife asked.

I replied, "I think it looks like . . . no, it couldn't be. Well, let's check." There in our trusty phrase book was the translation: lamb's brains. Yuck! Who wants to eat sheep thoughts? Let me tell you, it's not something you want to have every night.

Though we laughed about it (and the waiter probably did, too), the dinner was just one more reminder that we did not "belong." Circumstances such as these often made us feel alienated and homesick, an experience called *culture shock*. The travel brochures neglected to tell us that we might feel disoriented and even depressed because of the unfamiliar pattern of life we would encounter in foreign territory.

University catalogues can be downright deceiving on that topic, too. Some give the impression that college life will be all football, parties, and beach volleyball. And that studying will take only a few hours a week. When not living the life of the smiling, insignia-covered students pictured in the collegiate "travel brochures," newcomers may find themselves wondering if the university should be sued for false advertising. Without exception, when grads hear that I call the initial adjustment into college "culture shock," they say, "Was it ever!"

Although the academic culture will be more like home than a foreign country would be, you will probably experience your share of culture shock. Without familiar surroundings, friends, schedules, and expectations, day-to-day existence can be transformed into a lonely, frightening experience. For example, take my freshman year. As I already mentioned, I was anxious to leave home for college. Although I enjoyed much of high school, I also hoped to begin a different life, to create a new reputation, and especially to have all the freedom that I desired. I discovered that taking advantage of that freedom can take up a lot of free time.

To put it another way, although I couldn't wait to wear whatever I wanted ("You're not going out of the house dressed like that!"), I wasn't ready to do my own laundry. Confronted with the Battle of the Laundromat, my clothes often resembled the disheveled look of "before" pictures in an ad for permanent press. Unfortunately, the same was true in other areas of my life. Bombarded with ideas as challenging as behaviorism and feminism, and activities as depressing as drunken stupors and cheating, my intellect and emotions were often in serious disarray. After four weeks on campus, I had already sent home a "college is hell" letter. My parents probably thought I was exaggerating (again) but my life did feel hellish. Plagued by doubts and disappointments, my faith was lying in the hamper along with my stinky socks.

Must the freshman experience always be like this? No. And mine was only temporary. I had great friend-making, mind-popping, soul-sailing days as well. Of course, some freshmen will adjust more smoothly than others, but especially at a large state school, one can easily feel like a loose bolt in the great clanking institutional machine. At a small Christian college, disappointment more often takes the shape of disillusionment when professors or fellow students fail to meet your expectations. Can culture shock be avoided? Not entirely. However, by considering the ways in which confrontations occur and examining strategies for coping with life's little quirks, you might be able to keep your clothes and soul a little less rumpled.

What can you know about the shape of your potential culture shock? In other words, what are you in for? In part, it depends on what college you have chosen. Although many of my examples will address the adjustments of leaving home to attend a secular campus, certain principles will apply to most situations. I attended a large state university, but now that I teach at a small Christian liberal-arts college, I have discovered that most students, male and female, contend with similar concerns. No matter what you do or where you go, you will almost certainly encounter a certain shock to your expectations: situations and ideas that challenge your current assessment of your self, friends, worldview, and relationship with God. For the rest of this chapter, a number of these "foreign" customs will be previewed. In several of the following chapters, the focus will be on responses to these concerns.

Culture Shock to the Self

It was my first day in English Composition 101. With a gleam in his eye and chalk dust in a straight line across the rear of his pants, the professor asked us to take out a sheet of paper and answer this two-part question: "Who am I? Why am I here?" With a rush of honesty, I wrote in the center of the next page, "You got me, pal!"

Was that so surprising an answer? If many at forty and fifty still don't understand their "identity," how much can be expected from the masses that invade the dorms at eighteen? Perhaps the most significant transition for new collegians is the movement from a world that was defined *for* them to a world that must now be defined *by* them. With few rules set out for them, freshmen must make decisions in a culture unlike the one they left behind. Some formerly loyal youth group attenders will find themselves drinking heavily for the third weekend in a row. Even diligent students can crack under the pressure to become a better student in a less-disciplined environment. Although I was a new

Christian at the time, some of my most riotous and soul-troubled times occurred during my freshman year.

In high school, there is a certain security in the variety of fairly well defined groups: the In Group, the Out Group, the Out-on-Purpose Group, the Hard Guys, the Soft Girls, the Too-Smart Group, the Jocks, and on and on. Of course, once away from home, the labels change or become meaningless. And that also goes for the labels you've set up for yourself. No one in your dorm cares that you were a beauty queen or starred in *You Can't Take It With You* or got an "A" from mean Mr. Snorer or made that great catch in the final minute of the championship game. Having left behind the positive reputation builders as well as the negative ones, you end up asking all sorts of unsettling questions. At least for a while. Who am I? A Christian? (Or only a church-goer?) A jock? (But I can't make the teams here.) A budding starlet? (But I'm surrounded by so many spectacular flowers that now my thorns show.) A good student? (But so is everyone else or they wouldn't be in college.) What makes *me* distinctive?

Identity shock is not the only personal problem you are likely to encounter in your new culture. Stress may also wreak havoc on your psyche. As responsibilities multiply, so does tension. There's cooking and laundry (yikes!), budgeting (arrggh!), and little or no supervision (yippie!). Although some of you will not have to fix your own meals, all of you will need to manage money, studies, and time—as never before. Lack of supervision sounds appealing, but sometimes the "real you" who surfaces in private, unobserved moments is not the "you" you were hoping for.

The emphasis on freedom raises the issue of identity again. What do you do when no one you care about is watching? For example, few fellow students on campus may know anything of your Christian experience. Will you "take advantage" of your anonymity by fooling around with all the things you've been "missing" all these years? Invariably, this question: "What should I do?" (which you may think is wholly concerned with externals) will drive you deeper to a more fundamental, internal question: "Who am I?" Along the way, you may also ask, "What am I becoming?"

Loneliness may also become a stressful dilemma. Now I'm sure that *you* are likable, fun-loving, outgoing, dependable (not to mention thrifty, brave, clean, and reverent). However, maybe every once in a while you have a teeny-weeny problem feeling at ease with new people, especially those rowdy types that reside in the dorms. What does this have to do with being lonely? Sometimes people are lonely because they do not fit in. You may not be comfortable with the groups that have formed in your dorm or with their typical activities. For example, if you go to a secular school and don't develop Christ-oriented friendships, you may find yourself in the same situation as mine: uncommitted to Christian groups but too conscience-stricken to follow along with my other acquaintances. On the other hand, if you go to a Christian college, you may discover that the uniform smiley-faced niceness sometimes rubs you the wrong way.

On weekends I sometimes wandered around campus, feeling sorry for myself and trying to find a quiet place to eat worms. On a particularly slithery night, a group of earnest Christians tried to evangelize me as I was peering into a concert on campus. One of them made some inquiry into my spiritual status and I responded, "Yes, I'm a Christian. Now get lost!" I wasn't likely to win a scholarship to Mr. Rogers University.

Whereas some students feel lonely because they do not fit in, others get into trouble because of their excessive fear of rejection. One of the first times I spoke to a group on the subject of "Gearing Up for Culture Shock," one listener told me afterward how excited he was to be going to the University of Oregon. He was planning to single-handedly turn the campus "upside-down for Christ." His strategy must have been flawed, for a year later I discovered that he had joined a fraternity in which there were no other Christians. When his worries about being rejected by his fraternity brothers led him into the local party scene, he became addicted to cocaine within two months. This once-enthusiastic young Christian dropped out of school and took a year to recover physically and spiritually.

Others, particularly at Christian schools, have been disillusioned over the low level of spiritual, emotional, or intellectual maturity among their dormmates. A common refrain among these freshmen revolves around how fill-the-sin-in-the-blank could happen at a Christian college. On a less dramatic level, self-doubt may come to you as it did to Jennifer. Her loneliness stemmed not from a lack of friends but from the alienating shallowness of those relationships. Because so few of her friends seemed genuine or interested in a conversation beyond guys or clothes, she began to retreat into a self-pitying shell.

Identity problems such as these are not inevitable for all who climb the ivory tower. But even those who seem to step up with grace and confidence may find that the ladder wobbles, leans, or has a few missing rungs.

Culture Shock about Relationships

Okay, so instead of going it alone, you decide that conquering college life will be easier with somebody by your side. But who? For many, going away to college means the beginning of rich and varied friendships. (I know it's hard to believe that you might not always think of your favorite high school chum as your best friend.) Most of you will probably develop a cadre of new friends, and that means you must do a lot of discerning about relationships.

For most students, the biggest challenges come in those relationships they do not choose: roommates and suitemates. I tried to get close to my first roommate. It wasn't easy. He subscribed to *Playboy*, went to X-rated films, chewed tobacco, and partied, not until the cows came home, but until they—and he—threw up. Even the simplest conflicts can drive a person crazy. What if you are a slob, but your roommate is a neatnik? What if you love Twinkies and Chee-tos, but your roommate is a skinny-winny who would never lower herself to consume more than 1200 calories of raw vegetables a day? What if your roommate gets dates all the time and brings them over when you want to study?

Besides having to make such relational adjustments, you may encounter various culture shocks and aftershocks in the form of temptations to follow the crowd. Some of these temptations are straightforward; others are less con-spicuous and can catch you off guard.

Obvious Temptations

The snares that get a lot of press include sex, drugs, and becoming one of the Party Animals. These nocturnal beasts are often found snoring loudly in the most unusual positions. While seeking sustenance, PAs burp on all fours and forage for foamy liquid substances among the remains of the ash-strewn plastic troughs that are freely distributed in their natural habitat. Unfortunately, they are not yet an endangered species.

Besides glorifying rudeness, arrogance, and selfishness, Party Animals encourage the other more obvious tempta-tions of sex and drugs. There were a couple of "good ol' boys" on my dorm floor. In full control of their behavior on only rare occasions, they recorded their sexual conquests to compete with each other. As you might imagine, this edi-fying contest was the topic of many elegant and scholarly conversations in the lounge.

Will you be "safe" from these denizens of decadence if you attend a more conservative school? Perhaps. But no matter how sheltered your environment, any large group of people will include some who encourage you to "loosen up your uptight morals." Of course, some collegians *are* too rigid about things of no moral consequence. I have students who wonder if it is permissible to read a novel for leisure when they "should be studying the Bible." There are also those who cannot imagine ever breaking the unwritten dress code. Still decisions will have to be made in the moral arena. What about attending parties where alcohol is served and people are getting drunk? What about having one itsy-bitsy drink? Several? What about dating non-Christians or getting "sexually experienced"? What about R-rated movies? Pornography? What about checking out Professor X's stolen exam questions? The list could go on and on. And, *yes,* all these things do occur on Christian campuses.

Subtle Temptations

As difficult as these obvious temptations are, they may be easier to resist than the less flagrant forms of peer pressure that are dangerous to your spiritual health. The greatest challenge to Christian thinking and believing that exists in the collegiate arena may be the temptation to treat others the way your peers do, instead of the way the Scriptures teach. For example, here's a little test:

1. *Who is "a loser"?* Someone with no friends? A weird dresser? A guy with strange beliefs? Is this the kind of person whom *Jesus* would regard as a loser, or someone to whom *your friends* attach that label? What standards do you use? Is a loser anyone who doesn't act exactly like the rest of the cool, conformist crowd? Why do you find yourself at times turning your upper lip at someone? Because she is overweight? Or he doesn't like football? By modern criteria, Moses was deranged, the apostle Paul was a prude, and Jesus was a failure. But, as my professor of church history once said, "All of the saints embarrass us." Good questions for all of us are: "Who embarrasses me? Why? How do I treat them?"

2. *Who is "a success"?* Again, what are your criteria? Are your standards like Christ's? Do you change them for self-serving reasons? The Bible shows no respect for people strictly on the basis of beauty, power, money, or popularity. (Sure, Samson was a hunk and David was a king, but their stories are more about their faith than about physical strength

or royal status.) Why do you find yourself envying some of your peers and not others?

One way to check this kind of loser/success pigeon-holing is to reflect on your response when your friends ridicule someone. What do you say? Do you sometimes join in and treat this person as a soulless entity just asking to be victimized? When men or women are treated as sex objects, or when advisors are flattered for the sake of personal advancement, or when acquaintances are tolerated only because they provide a service (such as a ride downtown, advice on the next exam, or an "in" with someone you want to meet), these persons have been lowered to the status of "thing." The central commandment for relationships is violated whenever we do not love others as ourselves. We hate to be used, yet we often use others to get what we want.

In all of the above situations, the need is great for tough-minded attitudes and actions informed by the grace of God. Pressures to conform to the world's standards will tempt you to act as if you do not know God. You may begin thinking that today's choices don't matter in the long run, and that you can always change "next week." But the apostle John wrote, "Anyone who claims to be in the light but hates his brother is still in the darkness" (1 John 2:9). As long as we are on this side of heaven, the practice of discernment in the treatment of others will be a significant concern for all Christians. If sometimes you fail, take heart. The same apostle wrote, "My dear children, I write this to you so that you will not sin. But if anybody does sin, we have one who speaks to the Father in our defense—Jesus Christ, the Righteous One" (1 John 2:1).

Other tests of Christian fortitude will certainly appear, including the temptation to misuse time, to gossip, to let an evil practice continue by your silence, to blame others for your failures, or to lack integrity in dealing with your parents. The list is not complete, nor need it be, since one purpose of these sections is to help you to anticipate certain "typical" problems. Another purpose is to help you see that no matter what your circumstances are, you need a loving heavenly Father to guide, forgive, and sustain you. Will you avail yourself of his help and grace?

Culture Shock to the Mind

Of course, significant intellectual challenges come in college, but somehow these ought to be expected. For starters, there are three types of mental shock waves that can be pretty unsettling: the work load, the professors, and the ideas.

The Work Load

For most everyone except those in the top 1 percent of a high school graduating class, college-level coursework will be a noticeable step up in difficulty. For some of you, it will feel more like a five foot hurdle. How can you possibly manage your time so that all of the books get read and all of the papers get written before the end of the term or the end of your sanity? No more leisurely tossing spitwads at the clock. No more writing secret notes to hubba-hubba Hal Halfback during study hall. Homework and writing projects will definitely increase, sometimes to the point of the "If I Don't Finish This Paper by Morning I Think I'll Die" Syndrome (not to be confused with the "When My Professor Reads This Paper I Think I'll Die" Syndrome). If not treated, this condition may escalate into pathetic displays of All-Nighterisms: stale popcorn littered around a desk chair occupied by a sack of human flesh, every living cell of which is entirely asleep except for ten fingers moving feverishly across a keyboard and two bulging eyes propped open by force of nine gallons of coffee.

The Professors

Some professors are so tough they make Superman look like a Smurf. One literature instructor of mine, a 300-pound headhunter named Dr. Eli (who liked to remind us that "Eli" meant God), was once asked if he had read *Romeo and Juliet.* His response to this ill-advised question was to blast his chalk at 90 m.p.h. toward the innocent smile of the curious student. She ducked, and the chalk splintered into dozens of pieces with a resounding crack against the wall. We didn't ask too many stupid questions after that. In fact, we didn't ask any questions at all.

Professors also tend to be less directive than high school teachers. Once assignments are made, you may not receive any friendly reminders of due dates. Few professors will hound you for your papers. For the most part, you will be treated as responsible adults, which often translates to "If you flunk, it's your own tough luck." The intent here is not malicious. Professors rejoice in seeing good work as much as anyone else. The difference is that in college the prodding toward accomplishment must be more self-motivated.

Some students will encounter the phenomenon known as the Blatantly Biased Bickerer, whose presentations will be steeped in opinion and prejudice. Besides being confronted with lecturers who use the classroom as a forum for their latest pet peeve, collegians will typically experience a few zealots who are out for converts to their favorite "ism." Marxism, behaviorism, existentialism, feminism, who-cares-ism all have their faculty advocates. This is not so bad, really. Better to know where professors stand than to have them sneak up on you with their beliefs. However, some teachers have little patience with contrary views and may not look kindly upon open resistance. For example, during a History of Western Civilization course I took, Dr. Rundlesbumper assigned a take-home final that asked, "How has mankind progressed from the Renaissance to the present?" Thinking in moral and spiritual terms rather than along social or technological lines, I inquired, "What if I don't believe mankind has progressed?" Horrified by my heresy, he shouted, "Fine! But you better make damn sure you support that contention!" Spurred on by his defiant challenge, I threw myself into the task. Actually, he rather liked my fresh approach. When you least expect it, professors can surprise you by being human.

Professors at Christian colleges are not immune to bias either. Some have theological agendas, others favor certain programs. Most, if not all, have specific educational purposes in mind. Sometimes their goals coalesce into a classroom experience that is designed to encourage a student's pursuit of truth, but only after having numerous presuppositions challenged along the way. What if your Religious Studies teacher dismisses what your youth pastor presented as great theology? What if you learn that your most cherished verse is "not supposed to be translated that way"? In spite of these intellectual detours, the idea may be that unless you examine and even question your faith, it will not become a true path for living. All this is to say that even in the best of circumstances, professors can be unnerving.

The Ideas

Intellectual challenges to your faith will force you to confront the smorgasbord of beliefs that beckon temporarily at the philosophical buffet. As any smorgasbord frequenter knows, dishes placed alongside one another begin to look alike and even to taste alike. When so many philosophical options are available, as one quickly discovers in college, one begins to wonder what makes Jesus so unique. We are told that Nietzsche says this, Bertrand Russell says that, and Einstein suggests thus-and-so. It is hard enough to keep up with the differences between these thinkers, let alone compare their thoughts with Christ's. Since the Scriptures are not organized as a systematic argument, the Bible might seem to be an outdated, irrelevant piece of ancient history, about as tantalizing as a bowl of canned peas.

Even if still personally compelling, biblical truth may seem to be only one of *many* truths. You may have great difficulty trying to convince your skeptical peers that you believe in Christianity *and* that it is true. Christians who say,

"It's not true *because* I believe in it—it would be true if no one believed in it," are usually greeted with the retort "If it's true for you, great. But it is not true for me."

Whereas the plethora of theories about "reality" presented on a secular campus should come as no surprise, students at Christian colleges are often amazed to discover the variety of interpretations of cherished Scriptures or doctrines. To confuse matters further, especially at liberal arts colleges, professors are often reluctant to spoon-feed students with information they are "supposed to know." Students usually benefit from having to sort out the truth for themselves. But when ideas come quickly down the conveyor belt, the sorting process can be formidable. One coed recently remarked to me, "Here I am a senior, and I'm less sure of the truth than when I was a freshman. I'm familiar now with twenty-three theological points of view. When is somebody going to tell me what is the *right* one?" Although she didn't know it, the somebody this student was looking for, and kept missing, was herself.

Besides being confronted by an abundance of theories (which tends to water down the options), you may also be influenced by ideas that are so popular they have become as unnoticeable as the air we breathe. Although air seems too obvious to require our attention, there are times when ignoring its quality could mean disaster. For example, when the air is polluted, it begins to act like poison. On the intellectual level, too, we should be aware of any life-choking smog.

Unfortunately, few of us have been well trained for this task. Christians often spend significant energy analyzing and criticizing atheistic or cultist groups that are *obviously* hostile to Christian thought. While these efforts bear some fruit, by concentrating on the fringe elements we may miss some larger problems that more directly influence our ordinary existence. As we focus on the Moonies, we might miss the evils of Materialism. As we worry about the New Age, we may neglect the *Present* Age, with its fascination for whizz-bang gadgets and its tendency to desensitize us to such travesties as sexual violence or political incompetence. Our time will certainly be as well spent if we direct our efforts toward analyzing the values held by the average Joe or Jane.

Harmonizing the Parts

Those, then, are a few of the personal, relational, and intellectual challenges in the collegiate culture that may rise up to shock you. Among other things, such experiences will tend to leave you feeling troubled and even longing for the predictability of home. Or you may feel so "torn apart" that the words of the Scarecrow of Oz ring true: "Part of me is over here and part of me is over there!"

It is natural to question our commitment to people and ideas when we switch worlds. Sociologists have used the term "plausibility structure" to describe the principle that what seems reasonable in one situation may seem less believable in another. Within the confines of a certain environment (a youth group, for example), certain ways of believing and behaving (living according to Christian principles) make sense. When you leave that familiar structure, what was easy to accept in one setting may seem questionable. Suddenly, the security you felt about settled opinions evaporates into unsettled anxiety. You may confront such very difficult questions as: Was the faith of my high school days genuine, or only a convenience? Do I truly believe in Christ, or did I only play-act my faith because the youth group was fun?

In junior high I attended a Christian Science church. Besides the limited alternatives that existed when my parents dropped me off and did not return for an hour, my main motivation for being there was a pretty girl in my Sunday school class. When I stopped attending the church, I realized that I had a hard time believing what I had been taught for those few years. My "faith," such as it was, depended entirely upon the "plausibility structure" of the

Sunday school class. Once out of that environment, I ceased to believe (but I *did* date the girl for a while!).

Although the culture shock of college life can be troubling and wearying, your doubts and struggles can lead to a stronger, more mature faith. Not only are wise but feeble beliefs often made stronger when challenged, false and foolish ones may recede under the glare of hard truth and eventually be discarded. Once I left the familiar comfort of the Christian Science church, for example, I began a more sincere search for truth, and that quest led me eventually to Jesus Christ. To seek God in earnest is to learn that God is not necessarily impressed with people who can recite doctrine, quote Scripture, and practice churchly niceness once a week in a group setting. God wants our character—who we really are—to conform to his character every day in every way. Only then will our motives and behavior come into closer harmony with the way we were meant to be. Knowing him means becoming like him.

So far, admittedly, I have painted a pretty bleak picture of collegiate life. Is it really as dismal as all this? Yes and no. Some people find it even more difficult, but others adapt easily and enjoy every minute. The purpose of this chapter has been to prepare you for some of the more predictable conflicts. Since my wife and I had been warned about the shortage of ice cubes in Europe, we drank our warm Coke with dignity. If only we had been warned about *cervelle!*

What's in Your Heart?

1. What "culture shocks" have you encountered so far in college (or in some other new environment)?
2. Of the "temptations" mentioned, which ones seem most appealing to you? How do you deal with this?
3. Has your youth group served as a "plausibility structure" for you? Do you depend on the music or friends or "the message" to keep your faith going?

Faith and Morality 101

Love must be sincere. Hate what is
evil; cling to what is good.

Romans 12:9

With a sly smile, Roxanne coos softly,
"If it feels good, go ahead."

"Yeah," says John, "be your own best
friend."

"Shouldn't we think about this first?"
you respond.

Roxanne, attempting to ease your
doubts, adds, "C'mon, as long as it doesn't
hurt anybody else, it's fine."

"Sure," John agrees. "Whatever's
right for YOU."

"I suppose it's okay," you shrug.
"But—"

In unison, John and Roxanne inter-
rupt: "Just do it!"

How many times have you heard (or
quoted) those reasons for indulging in

questionable behavior? You have probably even wondered, "Couldn't they be true?" It would be less confusing if there were a trusty phrase book to translate the main ideas and implications of each popular moral slogan. For example,

"Just Do It": A handy phrase that can mean just about anything. To the would-be but fearful adventurer, it means, "C'mon, take the risk. Go for it." However, to the would-be libertine, it means, "Don't be such a fuddy-duddy. One little [whatever is in question: sex, drugs, theft, etc.] won't matter. Your mama ain't watching."

If you want to be faithful to Christ, the problem of sorting out when to "just do it" and when *not* to "just do it" will confront you often. In fact, given the challenges that collegiate life presents, this kind of moral crisis can happen daily; yet most students discover that the trusty phrase book that worked well in high school is no longer adequate. And a new and improved phrase book won't do. This time you'll need to truly know the language if you want to pass Faith and Morality 101.

Although that idea may bring back horrid memories of foreign-language videos *("repitan, por favor"),* it is the key to discernment. If you want to "be in the world but not of it," you need to evaluate every collegiate norm in light of the way Jesus would have us live. Before the later chapters investigate more specific issues, such as identity anxiety, dating, or doubt, this chapter will outline a way of thinking through any of the difficult faith-and-morality decisions that will face you at college.

What motivation should undergird a Christian's lifestyle? What are we all about? Are we simply moral do-gooders, in the worst sense of the word? Can we have faith and not care about our moral actions? Can we act morally without having faith? How do we sort out the interaction between morality and faith and become fluent in the language of "Should I or Shouldn't I?"

An Ethic of Discriminating Love

Before you proceed, it might be wise to get in your mind a specific moral dilemma or faith crisis. Are you wrestling with sexual problems, holding a grudge, or fighting with your parents? If you apply the following analysis to your particular situation, its meaning will become more readily apparent.

To say that the Bible's language is "love" would be to say nothing new. But what do we really know about love? Too often we use "love" to define "love," saying that "to be loving is to act lovingly." Where is a good definition when we need one? I believe Paul indirectly supplies one in Romans 12:9: "Love must be sincere. Hate what is evil; cling to what is good." First, Paul affirms that real love is not phony. A "sincere" love is genuine and without hypocrisy; it does not say one thing and do another. Paul also implies that love must be discriminating. It distinguishes between good and evil, clinging to the one and hating the other.

Whoa! Haven't we been told *never* to hate, only to "dislike"? How could "hating" be a godly quality? Isn't hate the opposite of love? Paul seems to be suggesting here that hating evil is a part of love. How could this be?

To hate evil is to recognize that which is destructive to love and to name it, disdain it, and resist it. If we see clearly, we cannot overlook evil, much less say, "Oh, well, wasn't that nice?" To love everything is to love nothing. It eliminates discernment. In an absurd example, two parents are talking about their children. The mother looks admiringly at her son and says, "Isn't he wonderful for working so hard at school?" Her husband adds, "Oh, yes. And I even love the way he hits his sister over the head with his baseball bat." Loving parents don't say that. They love their children but distinguish between their good and evil behavior.

Another example: Rod leaves a theater and says, "I *loved* that movie, every part of it." What does he mean by "love"? What about the part where revenge was glorified? What about the scene during which sex was treated as a way to make friends? We must *distinguish* in order to love. In fact, if we don't hate evil things such as famine, pornography, cruelty, or gossip, we are not loving those who are hurt by them.

Of course, "hating evil" does not capture the whole meaning of love. Paul also tells us to cling to the good—to accept, enjoy, and pursue all that is part of the good. Two varieties of "clinging" can be discovered in the image of a young couple's sailing adventure. One morning they board the boat, clinging affectionately to the ropes and mast as they prepare to embark. They love to sail and are devoted to the boat. After an hour or so of tacking back and forth and watching the gulls, they get caught in a fast-moving storm. The wind rages on and on and finally the boat capsizes. Now they cling to the boat, not out of devotion but out of desperation. So, too, we cling to things for a variety of reasons, some of them self-serving. We may cling to something (or someone) out of devotion, because we adore it, desire it, or hold it in high esteem. We may also cling to something out of desperation, because it provides safety, security, or refuge. What we cling to might be good or it might be evil. Also, the *way* we cling to it might be good or might be evil.

Defining Moral Choices

How can we exercise "moral" behavior that is true to the faith we claim to hold dear? If we define our moral choices according to the love ethic described by Paul, we have essentially four possibilities. We can (1) do evil and cling to it; (2) do evil, but hate doing it; (3) do good, but hate doing it; or (4) do good and cling to it. Each will be explored as a grammar lesson in the language of morality.

Do Evil and Cling to It

Certainly you have been angry once or twice with some practical joker who dumped frog intestines in your thermos or, more seriously, with an insensitive type who told tales behind your back. As you reflected on how to get back at these persecutors, did you plot, scheme, and delight in your anger, not wanting it to be interrupted? This, then, is the worst of the four options: to enjoy wickedness, to revel in it, to relish it, to look forward to it.

Given this definition, you probably have a hard time seeing yourself following this route. You are no more Adolph Hitler than you are Tinkerbell. (Of course, you have never had absolute power over an entire country. Who knows what you would do?) But you will misunderstand this category if you think of stereotypical villains only. Perhaps most of us have seen so many media-generated monsters that when we cling to evil, we "do not even know how to blush" (Jer. 6:15). For example, have you ever settled into anger so comfortably that you enjoyed every minute of telling someone off? Or sat in a dorm room and watched a pornographic video with rapture and delight?

As mentioned earlier, "clinging" can be thought of in two ways. If we cling to evil out of devotion, we will truly enjoy evil, resist giving it up, and defend our actions to all critics. Many modern performers take pride in being cruel or lewd. Just as some businessmen flaunt their deceitful means to get sales, some students cheat and brag about it. But we might also cling to evil out of desperation. Perhaps you have been caught in certain kinds of evil out of habit or lack of awareness, not out of sheer enjoyment. It may seem like the only way to get by or to cope with insecurity. The campus sleaze who is sexually promiscuous to "feel loved," or the blowhard who compulsively lies to save face, or the local tough who drinks daily to escape personal agonies, may think they have no real alternative. On a less dramatic level, destructive habits such as biting sarcasm or manipulative deceit might become desperate ways of surviving difficult circumstances.

Do Evil but Hate Doing It

Some might consider this option to be the worst of both worlds, because "If you are going to do what is wrong, you might as well enjoy it." Whereas this might be true for those who hope to get better at being bad, it is certainly unacceptable for those who would like to be faithful to Christ. Actually, doing evil and hating it is a huge improvement over doing evil and clinging to it. Although most people would not be able to detect an observable difference between the two, hating the evil we do at least gets us thinking in the right direction.

When we do evil but hate it, we are seeing evil for what it is: a sinister and ugly thing, the antithesis of all our loving God represents. Without this realization, there is little motivation to improve. Since much of the time we are ignorant of our sin, the painful discovery of the hurt we have caused or the depth of darkness within ourselves can spur our desire to change. One problem here is that although we may realize we are being unloving, insensitive, or quarrelsome, we may have a difficult time changing our ways. Who among us finds it easy to turn the other cheek or love pestering nags?

Paul admits, ". . . I have the desire to do what is good, but I cannot carry it out." Then he says, "What a wretched man I am! Who will rescue me from this body of death?" (Rom. 7:18b, 24–25). The advantage of a moral predicament is that it inspires improvement and faith. As Paul recognizes, when we see the need for redemption, we seek help from our Redeemer, and our faith therefore grows. Jesus is sympathetic with our struggles. He knows what temptation is like and how frail we are. Doing evil and hating it is not a call to wallow in constant guilt. Instead, we can take our agony to the Lord, who endured the ultimate agony, and we will receive grace.

Do Good but Hate Doing It

Is this getting too picky? Who cares how or why we are good as long as we are good? For one, the Bible teaches that *God* cares. From God's perspective, this option may be worse than the previous one, because the former implies true faith and the potential for moral change. The latter apes the religious and moral hypocrisy of the Pharisees. Doing good and hating it is self-righteousness.

Suppose you are at a fraternity party. As you approach the refreshment table for the fifteenth time, you notice that there is only one delectable danish left on the tray. You also notice that another party-goer is making her way toward the table. With great fanfare, you bow and let her have the last treat. But why have you become so magnanimous? Do you really want to serve this person? No, you are secretly angry with her for her incredibly poor timing. However, you smile and follow Miss Manners' Rule #26. The coed says "Thanks." And you say "No problem." Under your breath you add, "You pig," and then head off to get some Twinkies at the corner store. (Or, if she's cute, you may hang around a while, hoping your gentlemanly action may win you a date.)

We hate "doing good" (or "avoiding evil") whenever our motivation is more self-serving than genuine—as the above example shows. When we do good to save face, we are indeed loving with hypocrisy.

There are at least two basic reasons for choosing "good," and these two reasons do not always overlap. First, there is the good we do to benefit society, actions such as philanthropy, respect for the law, and peaceful behavior toward our neighbors. Second, there is the good that is motivated by a love relationship with God. Although it is socially preferable to avoid murder, God is not satisfied with restraint alone. If the one who avoids murder burns with rage, the social good is accomplished, but the individual's soul is becoming more vengeful. Or, if the one who avoids rape imagines the seduction in his mind, he is becoming more lecherous. Since God is at least as interested in the spiritual being we are becoming as in the kinds of acts we have committed, he reserves his harshest criticism for those who create the appearance of good works while festering in hatred, lust, malice, or selfishness. Jesus said to the Pharisees, "Woe to you . . . you hypocrites! You clean the outside of the cup and dish, but inside they are full of greed and self-indulgence" (Matt. 23:25). Doing good and hating it may seem an improvement over doing evil and hating it, but it may actually be worse. It is a lie.

Your heavenly Father is not working in your life merely to help you promote the social good. He is concerned with your soul, because he knows that what goes on in your heart will sooner or later make its way into your behavior.

This doesn't mean that since your "heart is not in the right place," you might as well commit the deed. If you hate me and wish to kill me, I'm glad that you don't. But even though much social good is achieved (and this is not to be scoffed at) God is not satisfied with mere restraint. If you think that outward obedience is all that God desires, you are equating faith with moral legalism. Following Jesus is not about following rules and keeping a clean ledger, as if God were a cosmic Santa Claus. Heaven is not for those who have kept a spotless record. It is for those who are becoming transformed into his likeness, by his grace. We become more like Jesus to the degree that we trust in our Father and do good because we want to act like members of his family. If we abide in him and he in us, we love even as he loves. And love without hypocrisy also means that it will be out of character to "do good but hate it."

Do Good and Cling to It

The highest spiritual choice, the way to imitate Christ most closely and provide a foretaste of what you are becoming, is to do good because you *love* doing good. As with the other three possibilities, this option is not quite as simple as it sounds.

There are two reasons to cling to the good. You may cling to the good, not because you enjoy it, but because it is the best you can do for the present. Out of desperation, perhaps, you love your neighbor and perform loving acts to escape the alternatives of bitterness or a critical spirit. "Desperate clinging" may be a necessary first step on the road to your final destination. If you *act* like you love your neighbor, you often find that you indeed love that person. Loving actions often lead to loving attitudes.

Finally, the highest, noblest, most Christ-like choice is to adhere to the good because the good is actually preferred. Can you imagine doing something merciful because you can't wait to do it? Holding your tongue because you love harmony? Giving money because generosity is fulfilling? Though you may see these goals as out of reach, you already act like this about some things. What happens on those Christmas mornings when you have worked hard on choosing or making the perfect gift for someone you love? You are more excited about giving than about anything else. What if every good act gave you as much joy as watching people you care about open such presents? What if you did good and held fast to it because it was so wonderful that nothing seemed better in your eyes? This is a preview of what you are becoming when you follow Christ: a member of God's family who has no conflict between what is good and what is enjoyable.

Loving without hypocrisy is the language that unifies faith and morality. Since all good comes from the Father, moral choices reflect the depth of our faith. If we trust the Father, we will do as he says, and someday we will be able to love him with all of our heart and soul and mind and strength.

If you didn't do so as the previous discussion unfolded, you might find it worthwhile to stop now and walk through each of these four choices with a particular moral dilemma in mind, whether it involves your parents, your studies, your sexuality, or your relationships. Clarity about options can save you a lot of grief in college. How you handle both the obvious and subtle temptations on campus is more important and complex than maintaining some sort of pious facade. As you get to know God, you will learn more about your inability to make these choices without him. As you trust his goodness, you will see him at work in you, helping you to enjoy doing good. C. S. Lewis summarizes well this combination of faith and morality: "Though Christianity seems at first to be all about morality, all about duties and rules and guilt and virtue, yet it leads you on out of all that, into something beyond. One has a glimpse of a country where they do not talk of those things, except perhaps as a joke. Every one there is filled full with what we should call goodness as a mirror is filled with light. But they do not call it goodness. They do not call it anything. They are not thinking of it. They are too busy looking at the source from which it comes."

What's in Your Heart?

1. What is evil? Give three or four examples. For each example, list two ways of hating evil that are appropriate and two ways that are not.
2. How consistently do you make each of the four moral choices explained in the chapter? In other words, in what areas do you:
   (a) Do evil and cling to it?
   (b) Do evil but hate doing it?
   (c) Do good but hate doing it?
   (d) Do good and cling to it?
3. How do God's grace and your faith relate to these moral choices?

Part Two
The Angelic Beast in the Mirror

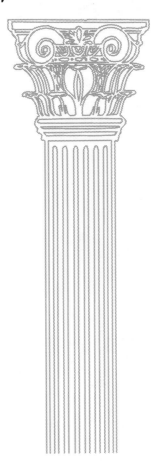

5

My Basic Problem Is That I Take Me Wherever I Go

Why is it possible to learn more in ten minutes about the Crab Nebula in Taurus, which is 6,000 light-years away, than you presently know about yourself, even though you've been stuck with yourself all your life?

Walker Percy

Who is the person you know most about? *Yourself,* right? On the other hand, who might you think is the person you know least about? *Yourself, again.* Hmmm. Example: You go to the mirror and see a face you've seen a thousand times, but now there's a mark on your nose that dramatically alters your appearance. You ask your sister, "When did I get that mark?" She replies, "Are you kidding? You've always had it." Hmmm, again.

If ever there was a paradox, it is you. (And, of course, me—and every "me" that exists.) Every human is an unpredictable combination of the known and unknown, elegant and earthy, abstract and practical, noble and perverted. Each of us can be the very best and the very worst of creatures, part angel and part beast. Yet we don't seem to know how to resolve or even investigate the tension. A researcher at UCLA, who has studied the attitudes of college freshmen for years, says of the latest crop: "The saddest thing of all is that they don't have the quest to understand things, especially to understand themselves."

Quest or no quest, college experience tends to turn people into raving introspecto-maniacs. You may not actually be asked, "Who are you?" on the first day of class, but you will be asked that question more subtly and quite often—in classes, in dorms, in friendships. Literature professors will ask you to discuss which characters in *Oliver Twist* appeal to you and why. While you chomp on a hamburger made from an oppressed cow who was raised on grain that could have fed hundreds of hungry people, a biology grad student will ask about your commitment to the ecology of the planet. Your roommate will want to know how you can be concerned about the homeless when you have thirty pairs of shoes. You, too, will find yourself wondering about your "self."

My students have at times revealed to me the circumstances that prompted their own identity introspections. Here are a few of their stories:

> Marcie walks into my office and declares that she wants to be a broadcaster. Innocently, I ask, "Why?" She ponders for a moment and then says, "Maybe I shouldn't be one, huh?" I'm left pondering her sense of who she is.
>
> In August, Heather's best friend dies in a car crash. Ten months later, her fiancé is hospitalized for six weeks in Zimbabwe while on a missions trip. She asks, "Why me? What is it about who I am that God is making me go through this?"

Dan and Becky find themselves in a whirlwind romance. After feeling and thinking things unfelt and unthought before, they make a commitment to each other. Soon they are physically involved. But two months later, they are fighting, saying, "I thought I knew you." Dan questions how he could have ever thought of himself as a "loving person."

Derek is a senior. During a lecture about education, he suddenly realizes that he has never learned anything for any reason except "to get by." His whole life in school, which is to say much of his entire life so far, seems like a waste because of his own low standards. He broods about what he has missed and the kind of person he is: someone who squanders opportunities.

Elizabeth is obsessed with good grades and skinny legs. After her first "C" and three "eat yourself to better grades" candy bars, she thinks about her loneliness and whether anyone will like her when she is both stupid and fat.

While studying for finals, Kristin learns from her mother that her sister has announced that she is a lesbian. She is shocked and saddened. Where can she turn? The family that had given her a sense of self was falling apart. She also has little sense that God is near.

These types of struggles often reveal to us something new about ourselves. It is usually when our resources are stretched beyond their limits that we are left with the question, "Just who am I?" Although most of you could answer that question with some clarity, how quickly, deeply, and accurately could you name three of your strengths and three of your weaknesses? Does your self-portrait have as much to do with image as reality? Do you define yourself in terms of some role such as Lady Killer or Cheerleader? Perhaps your answer is so shallow that you would laugh (or weep) if someone else gave it. "Let's see, who am I? I'm a Pepsi-fanatic. And I'm a surfer with a particularly soft spot for puppies and kittens." Or is your sense of identity so tied to a particular environment that to change surroundings would be to watch your identity collapse? You are Miss Cool around the English students; Miss Panic-stricken around the science crowd. Are you a bundle of contradictions? For example, are you intolerant of others' shortcomings, yet incapable of exercising the simplest self-control? In varying degrees, most of us find ourselves in these kinds of tensions.

There is another place besides the local counseling center where you can get some help with these dilemmas. Throughout the Bible are many stories that explain the mysteries of human nature. If we look at our reflection in the Scriptures, we will more fully understand that angelic beast we all see in the mirror. In fact, we need go no further than the first three chapters of Genesis to discover human paradox.

The Angel in Us All

> Then God said, "Let us make man in our image, in our likeness, and let them rule over the fish of the sea and the birds of the air, over the livestock, over all the earth, and over all the creatures that move along the ground."
>
> So God created man in his own image, in the image of God he created him; male and female he created them (Gen. 1:26–27).

In one rich and wonderful phrase, "God created man in his own image," we are informed of at least three telling truths.

First, it was God's idea to have humans around. God thought us up and decided we were worth adding to his universe. As the eloquent saying goes, "God don't make no junk." Since we were created by God, we are not a mere speck in the evolutionary firmament. We have meaning. Our dependence upon God is of the highest order; so, too, ought to be our thankfulness.

Second, being created in God's image also means that we are like him in some ways. Last time I checked, I was not all-powerful or all-knowing (I can't even manage my checkbook, much less the universe). So something else must be going on here. Although we do not have the extent of

God's powers, we possess qualities that are consistent with his nature. It's a bit like the way one of your own "creations" (say, a story) has a lot of you in it but cannot compare with the totality of who you are. In the same way, we are like God. Because there is a lot of him in us, we are "persons." We have emotions and can reason, create, and make judgments in the moral realm. (In Genesis 2, we see Adam exercising all these qualities: creatively naming the animals, reasoning about their unhumanness, feeling loneliness, and then relief and awe over Eve's creation.)

Third, and ultimately most important, being created in the image of God means that we are capable of relating to God. He has created us with a mind that can comprehend and communicate, a heart that can feel, and a conscience that can discern. I do not know why God decided to create us and put up with all of our rebelliousness, but I do know that he loves us more passionately than any parent, which is perhaps the closest human counterpart. New parents, especially, are pretty remarkable. Maybe you know a few of these otherwise sane folks who actually have *chosen* to get up all hours of the night to cradle a trumpeting babe in their arms, catch spit-up on a cloth, and dump little droppings into the toilet. Parents have an irrational commitment to look out for their offspring, come what may. God has chosen not only to put up with a lot of fuss, but also he still pats us to sleep and tells us to look both ways when we cross the street. I suppose he perseveres for the same reason that any loving parent does—he wants the best for his kids. Is it any wonder that we are called *children* of our heavenly Father? It is our privilege to be adopted into the family of God, to be like him, to be known by him and to know him. And, for a brief and shining time we "felt no shame" (Gen. 2:25).

Then Came the Beast

If the story stopped at the end of Genesis 2, we would have no problems about identity. But before even a slow reader could settle into images of unending Paradise, along comes Genesis 3. You all know the story. The Lord God gave Adam and Eve everything that he had created. All the animals and plants in a perfect world were theirs, all except one tree. Only one tree. This is not unlike getting a free trip to Disneyland with no waiting in line, but you are forbidden to go on Space Mountain. Although it's a nice ride, you could live without it, especially since everything else is yours. So what would you do? Like any other curious soul, you would run over to the ride, because it must be really something if it's off-limits. And so did Adam and Eve.

After a little persuasion from a self-appointed nurseryman, our friend Mr. Snake, the first couple decided that Paradise wasn't enough. They wanted more. They wanted to be in charge. They wanted knowledge God wouldn't give them. As it turns out, what they wanted was hell. So sin entered the world, and there's a beast in all of us. The image of God is fogged up, tinted, cracked, not fully operative. No matter what we do, we cannot free ourselves from the reality of being born sinners in an imperfect world. This is a familiar though perhaps worn-out phrase. A contemporary translation is that we are so constitutionally flawed that we cannot achieve the truly good in motive or deed; we are inclined toward evil. Not a pretty picture. Before you can say "the devil made me do it," the Paradise envisioned in Genesis 1 had become a garbage dump.

The result of human disobedience is the existence of all sin, which is intimately related to the identity issues already raised. The serpent claimed that, if the fruit was eaten, "You will be like God" (Gen. 3:5). Just as the desire to be God ruined the first man and woman, our sin—our desire to be God—eats at us from the inside-out. Our sinfulness is a rejection of God as the center of the universe. Instead of serving him, we make choices that serve ourselves. When children whine and say, "I will not share my toy," they are actually saying, "I am the center of the universe." When adults say, in essence, "I will not show you kindness" or "I will not forgive you your insult," they are also trying to control their world by usurping the authority that belongs to God. The downfall of Adam and Eve is *everyone's* problem.

Let's take Mark, a fine young man, a bright lad from good Christian stock. After attending a Christian elementary school, he went to a public high school and received grades high enough to get accepted into a solidly Christian liberal arts college. His parents are thrilled because they believe he'll get a fine education and won't have the temptations of a secular university. Mark is pleased that he'll be able to get to know his professors in this relatively small school and that most of the student body will be excited about God. During his first week there, he learns that his suitemates say they are Christians but think that a Quiet Time is when you make a move on a girl; and they talk about and try moves he had never even imagined. Now he finds himself doing some of that imagining. And when his friendly professors all gave pop quizzes, Mark averaged two out of ten.

Next we have Amy, a fine young woman who has gone to public schools, not only because her parents could not afford private schools but also because they are not Christians. In fact, they are alcoholics and are also divorced. Amy, who became a Christian during her senior year in high school, can't wait to go to State University because (1) her parents will not be there; (2) she hopes to meet some other Christians; and (3) she wants to get involved in a sorority. During her first week of school, her roommate has come back to the dorm drunk every night (once with a male student who spent the night); her Christian hunting has yielded two weirdos in polyester suits; and she has been rejected by two sororities because (as one member told her) her hips are too big. At least her parents weren't there.

Mark and Amy, though not on Skid Row or on their way to jail, experience the consequences of the Fall everyday. Not only does Mark have to endure the crass language of his roommates, he must face his own vacillating reaction to their behavior. This leads to doubt, shame, and, at times, self-loathing. Otherwise, at other times, he recognizes his response may be self-righteousness. Sin affects who we are and our sense of who we are. If Amy feels that she is estranged from her peers and from God, she may run from the very resources that could help her. Her self-pity constrains her. Since the Fall, the wonderful qualities that come from being made in the image of God are not enough to guide us out of these types of difficulties. Living with the faults of others is not easy, but living with our own faults can be even harder. Not surprisingly, we feel adrift from God, others, ourselves.

The basic consequence of the Fall can be summarized in one vexing proposition: *My basic problem is that I take me wherever I go.* No matter how many times you change your environment—to the dorm or an apartment or into a new job or with a new roommate—the most dominant component in your setting will be you. And the "you" that you take along is a fallen human, someone who cannot always choose to do what is right and whose motives are, at best, suspect. Although you may be able to turn over a new leaf at college, each new leaf is still part of the same old tree, a tree grafted onto one whose fruit was forbidden, a tree infected with a disease that will eventually kill it if not treated.

What to do? Before you rush away from this dismal scenario and plunge into the vitality and promise of the Gospel, you need to come to grips with a few facts that will not entirely change this side of heaven. First, none of us will ever be completely released from our fallen natures. The beast remains. Yet, in a world that glorifies "self-help," we tend to ignore our fallen state. Second, the world is fallen, too. You should not be surprised to find shame, fear, conflict, pain, and moral confusion in all of your dealings with institutions, including ones that are prefaced with the adjective "Christian." Churches, Christian college, and Christian marriages are as likely to house sin as you are. But, by the grace of God, the story does not end here, as we will discover in the next chapter.

What's in Your Heart?

1. List three of your strengths and three of your weaknesses. Which list was harder to construct?
2. What part of your high school reputation would you like to leave in college?
3. How does the title of the chapter explain certain difficulties in which you now find yourself?

6 Putting the Good News First

Any journalist . . . would recognize [Christ's story] as news . . . and good news at that; though we are likely to forget that the word *Gospel* ever meant anything so sensational.

Dorothy L. Sayers

On "The Evening News," the bad news is usually highlighted and reported first, and good news is buried in some sappy story about a pet armadillo. But the gospel of Jesus Christ broadcasts the Good News as the lead story, although it never lets us forget the bad news of the tree in Eden. We have already reviewed two words that describe the human condition: *created* and *fallen*. Now we come to a word that completes the trilogy of terms basic to the Bible's description of humankind.

First, a review of the enduring news: To have been *created* by God means that we bear his image. No matter how often we lust or boast or gossip, we still reveal God's mark upon us. We can no more erase his imprint than we can erase our personhood. We can cover it up with abuse or twist it with self-importance, but even the most wretched of people on earth is still an image-bearer of God who might one day be a vision of glory.

Second, a review of the tragic news: To have *fallen* means that on our own we cannot hope to live out God's purposes for us. The more we attempt to live up to the standards of God's character and holiness, the more we see our own weaknesses, and we may choose to ignore them. Ever notice how the guy who nearly runs you off the road is not only oblivious to his rudeness but blames *you* for getting in his way?

Together, these two qualities seem to provide a balanced view of ourselves. As Blaise Pascal was fond of saying, we are part angel and part beast. He wrote in 1660: "There are in faith two equally constant truths. One is that man in the state of his creation is exalted above the whole of nature, made like unto God and sharing in his divinity. The other is that in the state of corruption and sin he has fallen from that first state and has become like the beasts." Pascal's premise was that if we combine these doctrines, we can refrain from arrogance even as we champion human accomplishment. Though this is true enough, a perfect balancing act is impossible. The reason, I think, is that these ideas are not merely perspectives that we can hold simultaneously but descriptions of events that occurred in chronological order. In other words, the glories of the created world have been damaged by the fall of humanity. We had better hope that there is a third act to this drama. As Milton put it, after Paradise came *Paradise Lost*, not the kind of place you want to linger in. Our hope lies in *Paradise Regained*.

A Third Word and a Second Tree

Finally, we come to the wonderful news: To have been *redeemed* means that this fallen self, which "does evil and clings to it," can begin to become a soul that does good and clings to it, especially the good called God. The long-awaited but now familiar news is the remarkable, unexpected, momentous event of the atonement through God's Son, Jesus Christ. Think of this story afresh if you can, by relating it to a modern scenario. Suppose you are among the homeless. Cowering from the public because of a gruesome skin disease, you wander the streets, enduring as best you can, hiding your affliction whenever possible. One day, a transient comes along and inspires you with tales of his former life as a physician in a great hospital. You tolerate his fanciful stories about patients and surgeries because you enjoy his friendship, especially the way he treats you as if your scars did not matter. Orphans, addicts, and other outcasts all come to hear his marvelous tales that promise health and healing. During one storytelling, he takes out a needle and, to your horror, draws a little blood out of each person there. Entranced and disbelieving, you watch as he stares at the needle, full of every disease and curse imaginable, and then injects the venom into his own veins. In minutes, the mysterious stranger dies. As you rush to his side with the rest of the crowd, you look around and see a field of healthy faces. Also to your amazement, your own skin is smooth and clean.

Our heavenly Father knows our suffering. Because he loves us and knows the wounds that have resulted from our link to the first tree, the tree of knowledge, he heals us by putting his wounded Son on a second tree, the cross. The first tree necessitates the second, just as the one wound demands another even more deadly one. More wonderfully yet, though the healing remains, the wounded Son has risen to be by our side today.

The Good News, the lead story that Jesus told and made possible, was that Death has died. After Jesus taught that sin was inside all of us, he died and rose again so that the Holy Spirit could get inside and do something about it. He demonstrated that the cycle of sin need not be hopeless repetition and that we could live forever. Most encouraging of all, Jesus said that we would be redeemed. What would eternity be if it only meant that we would continue living in our current condition? What if we had 5000 years to grow less patient every day? What if laziness could multiply for eternity? The salvation that Christ brings is not just about going on forever. It is a complete transformation of our very person, a metamorphosis from "bent toward evil" to "lover of God and goodness." As Frederick Buechner says, "The news of the Gospel is that extraordinary things happen . . . just as in fairy tales extraordinary things happen." The Good News of redemption is a fairy tale come true.

This is the inheritance that Peter speaks of in his first epistle (1 Peter 1:1–9). It is the ultimate infusion of Christ's spirit into our lives. It is the fulfillment of the promise that "someday I'll do this right," that someday we will be in heaven without shame or guilt and no longer distanced from God. There will be no more pain, conflict, or confusion— because the Paradise that was lost will be regained. When we are changed into sons or daughters of glory, we will be able to live forever with the triune God in his kingdom in Paradise. Now, that's something to *cling* to!

Of course, life with Jesus on *this* side of Paradise, while not perfect, can be rich and exciting. As I mentioned in my introduction, G. K. Chesterton describes the Christian life as a robust, romantic adventure, combining "the fascinating terrors of going abroad" with "the humane security of coming home again." Following God is *exhilarating* because he will keep us from complacency, *challenging* because he will use circumstances to develop our souls, and *consoling* because we know that he acts out of goodness.

Without Christ, we are trapped in our desire to be the center of the universe and find ourselves dodging the potholes on the road to death. If Christ lives in us, we are adopted into God's family and are under the tutelage of a loving Father. Then we walk with a guide along the road to life. As you might expect, this choice concerning death or life has a way of influencing not only your attitude toward education but also virtually every decision you will ever make.

Three Pressures and Some Redemptive Relief

Peter Haile wrote a book a few years ago called *The Difference God Makes*. The title got me thinking about how I have changed since becoming a Christian. I also considered the ways in which my life has remained the same and the ways in which I try very hard to keep my life appearing to be the same. If we truly believe that we have been redeemed, what kind of a difference will God make in our lives? More specifically, how does redemption affect how you handle the pressures you are likely to encounter in college?

Identity Thumping

One pressure will come as you evaluate yourself. You may say that you care deeply for others but discover that you are consistently insensitive. A potential romance may drive you to obsessive odor-checking and image-primping. As if puberty didn't give you enough grief, the college experience has a way of making your dim vision of yourself even murkier. Furthermore, it poses brain teasers that make you wonder if you really know yourself at all.

Your identity will get thumped in varying degrees as long as you inhabit that bag of skin with your name on it. It's normal to experience an occasional identity crisis, since, those who are entirely sure of themselves are probably not sufficiently introspective; they may even be dangerous. Even so, unless you want to spend your days wallowing in a muddy self-image, you need to get some grasp on who you are and where you are going. The "third word" informs these concerns.

To be "redeemed" means to have been rescued *from* something and brought *to* something else. The "from" is our cursed state after the Fall; the "to" is the family of God.

We are not naturally sons or daughters of God. We are adopted into his family which confers upon us an identity with certain traditions and values. A colleague of mine tells of growing up in a close-knit family. The last words from her father as she walked out the door were always, "And don't forget you're a Smith." Being a Smith was an honor that carried with it a certain knowledge of security, affection, and responsibility. How much more marvelous it is to be a child of God! As J. I. Packer says in *Knowing God,* "Do I, as a Christian, understand myself? Do I know my own real identity? My own real destiny? I am a child of God. God is my Father; heaven is my home; every day is one day nearer. My Saviour is my brother; every Christian is my brother too."

What difference should this adopted identity make in your life? Being a child of God means that you are in relationship with a loving Father who has taken you into his family to prepare you for an eternity with him. It means the security of knowing that you have been chosen and that you are loved. When your identity is thoroughly informed by this reality, you will think and act as a son or daughter of God. You will want to make choices consistent with what it means to be a child of God. Too often decisions are based upon spurious identity orientations such as pleasure-seeker or career-climber. For instance, why is your roommate planning to become a journalist? Is it because he wants to learn to communicate the truth about important events? Or because he wants to have power, impress his friends, and have access to privileged information and important people?

Perhaps those of us who come from scrambled families will have a weaker vision of what adoption means. The apostle Paul recognizes that all of us are sinners with tainted backgrounds. Yet he offers hope: ". . . when we were children, we were in slavery under the basic principles of the world. But when the time had fully come, God sent his Son . . . to redeem those under law, that we might receive the full rights of sons" (Gal. 4:4–5). Although we were all born deficient, Jesus' sacrifice liberates us to the status of rightful heirs to all the treasures of our Father's kingdom. "Little Orphan Annie" transformed many lives and *deserved* to be adopted. But God is no Daddy Warbucks. What *we* deserve is to be left behind at the orphanage. Because we can lay no rightful claim to our inheritance, we are the beggarly recipients of an adoptive Father's mercy and generosity.

In college, many roles will compete with this sense of adoption. You may try to establish your personhood through activities that announce you as "good student" or "entertaining friend" or "decent athlete" or "spiritually minded Christian." Or you may try to convince yourself that you are wonderful and worthy of the highest esteem. But what the Father has given you in adoption is an identity that is true, maturing, and meaningful. It is a "family name" that frees you from the tyranny of living to impress or please others. And yet it is a *gift* you neither deserve nor could earn on your own behalf.

Stress

During my freshman year, I took several courses with my friend Terry. We studied together, endured test anxiety together, and sweated through exams together. After each exam, however, the similarities ceased. Terry kept on sweating. He worried about each answer. Every day. Until he received the exam back. Then he worried about his grade. Terry had an ulcer by the end of his freshman year.

The stress of college life manifests itself in shapes peculiar to each student. Some can't handle freedom. Some can't handle responsibility. Students who have been able to coast along to decent grades in high school may be in for a stressful surprise. To compound matters, our society tends to set up images of perfection in body, skill, and thought that constantly remind us of our inadequacies. The implication is that we should be entirely self-sufficient, that to rely on anyone or anything is weakness. We end up feeling stressed from our toenails to our eyeballs, yet guilt-ridden because we are supposed to be perfect. This, of course, leads to more tension.

Instead of concentrating on not feeling stress, we can "do good and cling to it." We can imitate Christ, not our culture's superstars. We can exercise our faith by trusting the God who has adopted us. Sadly, the phrase "Just trust God" is often the Christian equivalent of saying, "Minx rewff Snik." That is, it says nothing. I wonder if "faith" is the most used and least understood word in our vocabulary. More on faith later. For now, our attention is focused on how trust in our Redeemer can ease the stresses of college life.

Redemption is, in part, a moral and spiritual education from the finest Tutor around. As omnipotent, all-wise, and loving Teacher, God is educating us through the interplay of our circumstances and our needs. Although we cannot expect a world of fallen people to be free from conflict, we can depend on God's supervision and instruction. And he sometimes seems to use unpleasant techniques. If you are drifting from him, perhaps he'll bring you back through some difficulty. Because "the testing of your faith develops perseverance" (James 1:3), hard as it may seem at the time, stress is a part of learning to trust God. Though we have been rescued from the lumpy oatmeal at the orphanage, our adoptive Father has a far more complicated agenda than supplying us with nourishing meals.

Stress also reminds us of our need for help. I like what my friend Charlotte says matter-of-factly when a difficulty or tragedy strikes: "Looks like we need a Savior." We sure do! Among other things, pressure is a reminder to step back and relax, to take ourselves less seriously. It is too easy to forget that God is in control, that the world won't disintegrate without our holding it together.

Loneliness

Joanne might wait twenty minutes for a friend she doesn't much like, rather than go to the dining commons alone. Because Brad has such a strong aversion to silence, when outside he always has his trusty earphones playing full tilt and when inside he always blasts the radio or his CD.

Julie is so worried about winning and keeping friends that she tries to be perfect in everything, especially her appearance. She is bulimic.

About people like Joanne and Brad, Pascal says that "the sole cause of man's unhappiness is that he does not know how to stay quietly in his own room." In our media-dominated world, many students would say, "Who would want to?" But Pascal's point is deeper. He is arguing that until we *can* be alone comfortably, we will remain unsatisfied, constantly seeking some diversion.

Why do so many people hate to be alone? Perhaps we see aloneness as a kind of judgment, a statement of our unattractiveness. In the movies, on TV, even in commercials, romance and friendship seem so natural. But here you are awkwardly bumping along, wondering why you never manage to be embracing some gorgeous creature in a field of flowers, even though you use the right brands of perfume and chewing gum.

I think most of us respond to being alone with either self-pity or an overeagerness to please. The woe-is-me syndrome can lead to a sense of disappointment with God for not "being close" or "meeting my needs." Or you might accuse yourself, saying, "My faith isn't strong enough; I didn't pray right." On the other hand, if you are insecure about who you are, you are probably excessively concerned about being accepted. Then it is easy to become a social and moral chameleon, even when it means a clear violation of God's Word. Either response means taking everything too personally, with the brooder multiplying the pain internally, and the people-pleaser spreading it out externally.

How can we go about coping with loneliness? Although there is no magic wand that can instantly wipe it away, our struggles with loneliness (and other problems) often revolve around our insistence that God take care of our needs NOW. We may view God as a supernatural fix-it man, a wizard for our worries. If we've been adopted by God, why don't we *always* enjoy the pleasures of being in his family? There is a

"Victory in the Spirit" theology that many try to apply to every disagreeable situation, but I believe this is not only unbiblical but leads to guilt and disappointment. The idea is that once we've been saved and are on the Road to Life, everything will be a Sunday drive, providing that we "stay on the road" or "live in the Spirit." I used to pray that God would "take away" my roommate problems or my sinful habits or even my car's oil leak. After many agonizing and seemingly fruitless prayers, I have concluded that God's primary goal is not to remove unpleasantness from our lives. He is not a genie. He is a Father—and he is trying to teach us how to trust him in all circumstances.

We don't like to "wait on God." We are glad to be redeemed, but we want all the benefits at *our* convenience and as fast as microwave popcorn or copy machines or liposuction. But, whether we like it or not, spiritual transformation takes time, as Paul told the Galatians when speaking of the qualities of godly life: peace, gentleness, self-control, and so on. He calls them *fruit* of the Spirit for a reason. Fruit needs time to mature. Who would have thought that from the little stick that was planted in my yard ten years ago, we would get a bounty of apples this fall? But I could no more rush that harvest than I can rush my spiritual ripening. We *do* get better. Paul assures us that "he who began a good work in you will carry it on to completion until the day of Christ Jesus" (Phil. 1:6). In the meantime, we would do well to trust in our adoption into God's family, knowing that we are his children and will ultimately act like we belong.

What does this have to do with your loneliness, the dorms, and Friday night pizza? Mainly that you may need to move from fearing aloneness to appreciating it. Since you are probably accustomed to silent tranquility only when the electricity shuts down, you may need to endure some discomfort until you learn that isolation is not necessarily desolation. The more settled you are about being in God's family—with all of the freedom and knowledge that adoption brings—the more accepting you will be about every circumstance the Father sends your way. Although you are free to try to change a situation, you are also free to be content with quiet Friday nights when everyone else is at the movies.

So this "third word," *redemption,* provides relief from the pressures of daily experience. Even the culture shock to the self can be substantially less startling if you understand and accept the reality of your redemption. If you don't, you are likely to substitute some skewed view of who you are and apply it to your struggles. Those facing an identity crisis often try self-praise as an answer to their problems. Those weighed down by stress find perverse solace in complaining that the world does not revolve around them. Those struggling with loneliness often blame themselves for circumstances well beyond their control. At best, these "solutions" will provide only short-term relief. Putting the *good* news of the gospel first, however, will provide some immediate help as well as the longest-term relief around.

What's in Your Heart?

1. How would you explain "redemption" to a smugly self-satisfied classmate?
2. How would you explain "adoption" to a depressed acquaintance?
3. Besides the theological responses of "redemption" and "adoption," what have you been taught (from parents, media, church, friends, etc.) about how to overcome identity thumping, stress, and loneliness?

Can I Love Me If I Know Me?

By the grace of God I am what I am, and his grace to me was not without effect.

1 Corinthians 15:10

In the best-selling children's book *The Magic Locket*, a little red-haired girl is transformed from a pathetic bumbler to a cheerful achiever because she believed in the power of a magic locket given to her by Great-Aunt Emma. When the curious child opened the locket one day, she saw nothing but her own face shining back at her from the mirror inside. She instantly knew that the only magic she would ever need lay within herself.

A common enough sentiment today. We often hear that weak self-esteem is the cause of everything from race riots to low SAT scores and that strong self-regard is

89

the foundation for attaining mental health and stable relationships. What counselors and pastors alike usually mean by this is that we should love ourselves more. We ought to be our own best friend, because "you can't love anybody else until you love yourself." The logic seems to be that if we all felt terrific about ourselves, the whole world would get along quite swimmingly.

There is a certain intuitive attraction to that idea. For example, people who fail one exam and are depressed over their incompetence for a month are rarely pleasant to be around. The folk wisdom at this point is that the way out of the sense of abomination is to concentrate on finding things about ourselves to love. If we are tipped in the direction of feeling bad about ourselves, the scales would come aright if we could convince ourselves how "okay" (or even "great") we are. I've heard students say, "I'm going to work as a camp counselor this summer because I know that it will boost my self-esteem." Or, "I can't believe how good I feel about myself." I've heard this Gospel of Self-Esteem preached by men as diverse as Robert Schuller and Phil Donahue, but I haven't seen it in the Scriptures. Bible writers seem to have a different word for it: pridefulness. It is one thing to *accept* yourself as a creation in God's image, an object of his love. It is quite another thing to *love* yourself self-consciously as a delightful work of art.

As much as I'd like to think that I'm sweeter than a chocolate hazelnut truffle, I can't seem to escape the reality of sin. The Bible says that sin reveals our desire to usurp God's authority. God's ego can handle being the Center of the Universe, but we are more than a little over our heads when we put ourselves in that role. Another way to put it is that the very essence of sin is arrogant self-preoccupation. If the self is naturally corrupt and sorely in need of redemption (and adoption out of desperate circumstances), why should I love it? Or, perhaps more aptly, *how* should I love it? What part should I love? Am I to love all of me, including my inclination toward evil? What does it mean to love myself? Does it mean that I am basically okay, morally above average, spiritually fit? If so, why did Christ die on the cross? True, Christ died because he loved us and felt we were worth dying for—but his death was necessary *because* we are sinners. To listen to the self-esteemers, one would think that Christ died because he couldn't bear to live without our wonderful, charming, prefect selves.

Didn't Jesus *Command* That I Love Myself?

Poor Jesus. If the atheists don't distort him, some of his disciples do. The Bible does *not* teach us to love ourselves. There are only two "great commandments" listed in Mark 12:28–31: "Love the Lord your God" and "Love your neighbor as yourself." That latter phrase, "as yourself," is not a third command, but a guide to the method for loving our neighbors.

In this passage Jesus is assuming that we take care of ourselves. Don't I make sure that I eat? That I am clothed? That I get out of the way of NFL running backs? Of course I do. The command here is to take care of others as you tend to take care of yourself. However, you miss the point if you merely give what you like to receive, as if everyone were encouraged by the same things. If you surprise your diabetic roommate with chocolate, you had better hope that it was the thought that counted. The call is to discern what another person's needs are and thus what would be the most loving way to behave toward that person. Isn't that the way *you* enjoy being treated?

Our basic problem in relationships is that we are too selfish and therefore neglect many opportunities to serve others. Who among us needs encouragement to be more self-centered? Anyone who has been around children knows that they must be taught to share. You won't hear many parents saying, "Billy, you are much too generous; please be sure to keep enough for yourself." I doubt that you'll need to tell your roommate to stop doing so much for you, either.

"Ah," you say, "but what about people who are so down on themselves that they are helpless in relationships? They make wonderful doormats, never protect their interests, and are trapped in a negative self-image." My point is that people who wallow in their own shortcomings ("Woe is me!") have the same problem as those who champion their accomplishments ("How wonderful I am!"). The sin in each case is a preoccupation with the self. The self-conceited person sees all events as revolving around her positively, as in: "*I* hope you know that I was the one who made things happen. To think that the professor noticed little ol' *me*." The self-defeated person sees all events as revolving around her, too, but in a negative way: "It's all *my* fault! If only *I* hadn't done *my* usual thing, everything would have been fine." In both cases, each "I" is playing a center-of-the-universe role. Sometimes even others-centered people may be morbidly consumed with their own indispensability. Yet, in the Sermon on the Mount, when discussing fasting and tithing, Jesus commends not the distraught martyr who seeks attention and sympathy, but the one who sacrifices cheerfully.

Because only God belongs at the center of the universe, we are rejecting him whenever we try to become "like God" in this respect. From Satan's perspective, any action of this kind will do. He does not care which avenue of selfishness we select as long as we attempt to dethrone God and crown ourselves in his place.

Humility: A God's-Eye View

The fact that center-of-the-universe thinking can manifest itself both negatively and positively explains the condition in which I usually find myself: I am often either congratulating myself or despairing of who I am. How can I be doing these things only five minutes apart? Because that is the essence of *all* sin: preoccupation with *self*. Truly humble people won't be worried about how much self-esteem they have or how much attention they are receiving from others, so they waste little effort boasting or roasting themselves. Contrary to popular perceptions, "humility" is not thinking poorly of yourself, sniveling around with a long face and saying about all your accomplishments, "Shucks, it was nothing." C. S. Lewis writes that the humble person "will not be a sort of greasy, smarmy person, who is always telling you that, of course, he is nobody. Probably all you think about him is that he seemed a cheerful, intelligent chap who took a real interest in what you said to him. . . . He will not be thinking about humility: he will not be thinking about himself at all." Humility is having a God's-eye view of ourselves, as neither a despicable worm who should be covered in salt nor a world-class saint. Paul advises us to consider others *better* than ourselves (Phil. 2:3). Hard to do when we're busy gazing at ourselves in the locket's mirror. What are the implications of this idea? In other words, how can removing our focus from ourselves help us answer the "Who are you?" question more satisfactorily?

Wishing Won't Make It So

The first desirable side effect of true humility has to do with getting better. Should those afflicted with poor self-esteem concentrate their efforts on loving themselves? I think not. Self-preoccupation will still be the basic problem. The word *self-esteem* implies an esteem that comes from within. If this kind of self-esteem is healthy, then complimenting myself should make me feel better. This strikes me a bit like the insomniac who is given the ill-conceived advice to cure the ailment by thinking about the process of going to sleep: "I'm falling asleep. There I go . . . oh, no I don't!" Just as an insomniac has to think of topics other than going to sleep in order to do so, those with poor self-images need to focus elsewhere if they are ever going to leave their self-preoccupation behind.

No matter where you fall on the scale from self-admiring to self-despising, you will need to learn to see yourself as God does: made in his image and therefore worth saving, but a sinner in need of redemption. Once again you can apply those "three words"—created, fallen, redeemed. "Self-image," if that term is required, would refer simply to the picture you have of yourself. Your main concern, as a pursuer of truth, is to have an accurate self-image, not necessarily a positive one. Christians can see themselves as persons loved by God, redeemed by God, headed for eternal life with God, indwelt by God's Spirit, and adopted into God's family. Nevertheless, though Christ lives in every believer, we cannot entirely trust our hearts. That is why, in our still-imperfect state, we so clearly need to rely on God. Your own self-esteem is not a trustworthy savior, but *he* is. Paul does not say "you in you, the hope of glory," but "Christ in you, the hope of glory" (Col. 1:27).

Humility gives us more room to be preoccupied with God and his world. As a friend told me, "You would worry less about what others think of you if you realized how seldom they do." Still, we can easily miss a certain paradox. Although the way out of self-preoccupation is not to glorify the self, some of us may need to go deeper into self-knowledge. Instead of striving for a self-image that merits such congratulatory comments as, "No wonder God loves me," Christians would do well to heed the classical prescription to "know thyself" or the biblical injunction to "examine yourselves" (2 Cor. 13:5). Not only is our insensitivity to others often due to our ignorance of ourselves, but we become even more shallow when we neglect the insight that can be gleaned through introspection. Self-denial does not require that we act as if we do not exist, but merely that we not insist on always getting our own way. As self-understanding increases, the self-impressed may discover reasons to doubt their sense of excellence and the self-depressed may uncover reasons to reject their melancholy.

Is Anybody Else Out There?

The second result of true humility is an improvement in our ability to empathize. If you are totally consumed by your own feelings and worried about how others regard you, there's not much room in your mirror for anyone else. The little red-haired girl may be happy about the world she's been introduced to through her magic locket, but it's a small world, indeed, if she's the only inhabitant. I've seen a cartoon picturing a room full of people, all thinking the same thing: "I wonder what they are thinking of me?" If self-preoccupation causes all events to be displaced by "me," sensitivity for others is diminished severely. On the other hand, a self-forgetfulness that stops short of self-obliteration permits us to focus on others and practice those rare skills that come readily to the empathic person: question asking and listening. As an experiment, during your next meal in the cafeteria, keep track of how many times you hear or make statements that are others-centered. Conversation can be remarkably self-consuming.

As obvious as it sounds, we all need to be reminded that the first step out of an obsession with our own importance is to spend considerable time and effort doing something for someone else. After five hours of planning a treat for someone that you love, your thoughts will be genuinely full of this person's pleasures instead of your own. But the cycle of self-centeredness will never be broken if you allow the face in your mirror to distort your vision of everything else.

Praise That Can Hide or Heal

A third implication of being truly humble relates to our use of praise. Under a steady stream of happy-faced stickers, and enthusiastic strokes, people can become difficult to motivate and desensitized to applause. Young children typically receive a multitude of magic-locket messages and "I'm terrific!" buttons for doing the most ordinary things in school. Above the entrance to a local elementary classroom is a banner that reads: "Through this door walk the greatest children in the world!" I'll grant that the parents would agree but isn't that a rather exaggerated claim—and a self-limiting one at that? How can everyone in the world be above average? If I'm extra special for being exactly as I am, why bother trying to be anything more? Although we are free to appreciate our dazzling and impressive human qualities, as well as our own distinctive gifts, we can recognize that value without laying on the flattery so thick that we raise a generation of smug and lazy underachievers.

While there may be a glut of superficial "Hoorays" in our culture, there is also a shortage of *meaningful* praise, the kind that acknowledges success but also encourages further effort, or the kind that draws attention to the unspectacular spiritual change. True humility leads to this depth of encouragement because to find out what would genuinely build up others, I need to think for a spell about them, to get inside their tennis shoes for a while. If I'm so busy sitting on my throne and admiring my gems and trophies, I may find it difficult to think about what others need. In a country of kings and queens, who will be willing to do the dishes?

The promise of the Good News can become the *best* news for your soul, giving you the building materials for an identity secure enough to take the risks needed to love others. The inquiry "Who are you?" is a vital, inescapable question that prods you to know the truth about God and yourself. Although your vision of spiritual things will always be a little distorted, you can make out the most important roadsigns and directions. As you learn more about yourself, you will find it easier to understand and relate to others around you, which will be the focus of the next few chapters.

What's in Your Heart?

1. Comment on this statement: "You can't love others until you love yourself."

2. What images come to mind when you hear the words *proud* and *humble?* Relate these descriptions to the discussion of humility given in this chapter.
3. In what ways have you been influenced by the emphasis on "self-esteem" in our culture?
4. How might true humility keep you from being naive about sin?

Part Three
Those Whom We Love

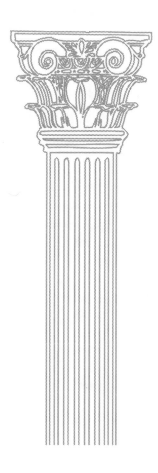

8

Friendship in an Age of Kleenex

[Jesus said:] "I have called you friends. ..."

John 15:15

So you finally make it onto your favorite quiz show, "Jeopardude." Trembling, you hear the final question, worth the Grand Prize: "Who was Chief Justice of the United States from 1874 to 1888?" In a panic, you think, "How can they expect me to know that?" As the host says, "Five seconds," your mind is blank, a clean slate, a nadir of nothingness. You start to say, "Wait a minute," but all that comes out is "Wait! Wait!" As your shoulders sink into defeat, the robotic host beams a 100-watt grin and says, "Yes, you've done it! You've won the Grand Prize! Morrison Remick Waite was our Chief Justice from 1874 to 1888! [I am not making this up.] And here to tell you about your prize is *Johnny!*"

"Thank you, Bob! Our Grand Prize for tonight is a gift well beyond your wildest expectations! You have won not a Rolls-Royce, not a cabin in Maine, not a million in cash, but—yes—you have won Chris McMahon of Oak Park, Illinois! That's right, you have won a friend for life, a loyal companion who will treat you like a family member, confide in you, give you encouragement and counsel, spare no expense to keep in touch with you, and sharpen you as iron sharpens iron! Brought to you by Kindred Spirits Catalogs. All this for playing 'Jeopardude!'"

You swoon, overcome with disappointment, "What do you mean Chris McMahon? You mean I don't get a car, a dream house, or designer clothes? Come on, I can get a friend anywhere!"

I know, I know, not a very plausible scenario, and hopelessly unfair as well. Since you would never expect to win a friend, how could you be blamed for being disappointed? Besides, wouldn't a game-show approach to friendship be just a little demeaning? All true, but the very improbability of the story raises some interesting questions. What do you count as important? What do you spend your time desiring? For what would you make personal sacrifices? What motivates your life-changing decisions? In a materialistic age, how is it possible to keep from living as if winning a lottery jackpot would solve all our problems?

In this first of three chapters on relationships, as we explore what it means to be a "good friend," I hope to encourage you to develop a quality of companionship that is uncommon in our times. Even more importantly, perhaps you will see friendship as a treasure that, as Samuel Johnson said, should be kept in "constant repair."

Daniel in the Lions' Dorm

Expectations about friendships are especially high during the first term on campus. Inevitably, disappointment occurs when roommates or suitemates "don't work out." If

potential friends prove to be untrustworthy, you may feel as if surrounded by hungry and predatory lions. Neighbors on your floor may blatantly disrespect your values and encourage you to do likewise by growling about your naive sense of resolve. Or you may have had a few disheartening conversations with suitemates who think that your faith is about as vital as yesterday's chewing gum. Because lions of all sorts prowl the dorms, it may seem sensible to either withdraw for fear of being eaten or seek to join the roaring pack.

On the other hand, you may have begun the strongest friendships of your life. Two months into my first college semester, I met Tom. We began to share meals, jokes, Frisbees, prayers, escapades, and dreams. We roomed together the next four years and were each other's "best man" in our respective weddings. Twenty years after we met, our families camp together and we still dream the dreams that made our friendship strong when we were no more than two lines on a grade sheet.

Even if most of the lions in your dorm are pretty tame, you may have begun to notice the hard truth that *kindred spirits are rare*. At twenty, this was less apparent to me than it is now, as I approach forty. Since friendships cannot be forced—they seem to "just happen"—I'm not suggesting that you work out a ten-step plan to go out and make friends (and keep them). Even so, I can look back and realize that my enduring friendships took real effort on my part, especially once "getting together" was made difficult by distance. Over a period of time, if my experience is any guide, "just happens" becomes "just deteriorates." In fact, many things conspire to make the maintenance of friendships difficult at the end of the twentieth century. If our appliances don't last beyond their warranty period, can we expect our friendships to persist?

Kleenex Relationships and Plastic Commitments

I am a bit of an oddity: a fourth-generation Californian. Since the West is primarily populated by rather recent pioneers, locals are usually surprised when they hear of my lineage. We are a mobile society, comfortable with transience, at ease with being on the move, and far more receptive to change than our ancestors. Wherever we go, we know we may not be there long. Employers often put in their want-ads: "Must be willing to relocate." We usually oblige, stoically reciting that "nothing lasts forever."

What difference does this make in our relationships? If we know that we will be moving on eventually, we will be reluctant to settle in, to think in terms of the long haul. Knowing that our friends may move on, too, makes us put up fences that discourage intimacy and openness. If we build only superficial relationships, we won't be very badly hurt when we are left behind. I remember a student of mine in a night class I taught years ago. During the break, she would immediately put on her earphones and listen to her cassette player. Who knows what greater listening pleasure might have occurred had she actually conversed with someone!

Because our easy mobility leads us to *expect* impermanence in relationships, we may not forbear much interpersonal conflict. Instead, we sneeze through friends like so many Kleenex, knowing we can always pull another one from the stack. One tissue seems as useful as another. Living in an age of disposable convenience inhibits perseverance and makes loyalty seem old-fashioned. We affirm the spirit of the age when we think we should be independent, self-reliant, indebted to no one.

Besides easy mobility, other factors contribute to the current lack of relational commitment that shows up in our resistance to long-term allegiances. First is *pluralism,* the availability of multiple options. The ice cream store has at least thirty-one flavors. Our televisions have dozens of channels. Many college catalogs describe hundreds of courses. Have you ever been sent to the store to buy something such as tomato sauce and had an anxiety attack because there were forty varieties to choose from? Although, for a consumer, pluralism means that we can experience the joy of pistachio-bittersweet chocolate fat-free dessert topping, it also tends to have a leveling effect. In other words, when we choose from three options, we can easily rank them in order of preference. With twenty-five options available, the task becomes so daunting that we lump most of the possibilities together, making them all seem equal. This is also true for friendships. You see so many potential friends in your classes that you conclude, "If this doesn't work out, I can always pick someone else." If you lived in a small town, your choice for friends might be between Michelle and Kara (or Joe and Graham). With only two possibilities, you might more readily learn the value of loyalty, for then the choice would be to work things out or have no friends at all. You are far less likely to conclude this at a college of 25,000 students.

Pragmatism—an orientation toward what "works"— is another conspirator against relational longevity. Americans love how-to manuals, efficiency tests, and performance evaluations. We want to know how we are doing, so we can improve what we are doing and see results *now* (or at least next week). From businesses to evangelism to romance, the pertinent question is "How far did you get?" When applied to friendship, this question asks "What's in it for *you?*" and inappropriately emphasizes efficiency, productivity, and a one-way system of rewards. Even asking, "Should I *invest* in this relationship?" betrays a pragmatic orientation, because it implies that unless you get a return on your investment you will seek another "portfolio."

Finally, *poor models* also make permanent commitment difficult to justify, much less achieve. Unless your parents are among the rare couples who are not divorced, or who do not act like they wish they were divorced, and have learned how to grow through conflict, you may have never observed a relationship that you would like to imitate. Given the pressures of modern life, it is no surprise that plastic slogans (let's do lunch) have become as common as loyalty has become uncommon. It is a testimony to the grace of God and the value of friendships that so many relationships persist as long as they do.

The Ingredients of Camaraderie

Commonality of Interests and Values

I have always marveled at the number of intellectual passions I share with my friend John. We seem to see life through the same pair of eyeglasses, smudges and all. For example, John and I admire the same authors, revere medieval sentiments and other "old things," and are vigorous defenders of education. It is almost eerie at times. But because we are kindred spirits regarding so many major and minor facets of life, we are "good friends" now and probably always will be.

The fact that John and I also resonate about the nature of discipleship makes our friendship even more rewarding. When I was a young believer, I thought I was supposed to have this sort of closeness with everyone in the family of God. I reasoned that all who were together "in Christ" would automatically enjoy each other's company and become great friends. Although it probably will work that way in heaven, I soon learned that relationships in the earthly (and thus still imperfect) kingdom of God are distorted by human frailties. Although we are called to *love* our neighbors, we need not suffer guilt because we find it difficult to *like* them all.

What separates those we love and truly like as *individuals* from those we "love" out of duty? When we see our vision shared by another, as I did with John, companionship grows into friendship. The great commonality that marks close friends is a very special bond. C. S. Lewis writes in *The Four Loves:* "In this kind of love, as Emerson said, 'Do you love me?' means 'Do you see the same truth?'— Or at least, 'Do you care about the same truth?' The man who agrees with us that some question, little regarded by others, is of great importance can be our Friend. He need not agree with us about the answer."

Sharp and Constructive Honesty

Besides asking similar questions of life, good friends go about answering those questions by "loving their friends as themselves." This love may sometimes call for brutal honesty, as Proverbs 27:6 reminds us: "Wounds from a friend can be trusted, but an enemy multiplies kisses."

Just recently I experienced this kind of well-intentioned pain. I had given a piece of writing to a good friend for review. Since his "lens for life" was so much like my own, I knew he would understand what I was trying to say and, therefore, that his criticism would be valuable. Although I had my doubts about the work, I was unprepared for some of the misgivings he expressed. I was wounded by several of his stinging comments. As I reflected on his critique of my work and of me, I came to see the unpleasant sensations as part of a needed surgery of hard truth, cutting into a part of me that I had hoped was not obviously diseased. After a short healing period, I reworked the piece, certain that it was now headed in the right direction. My friend could have flattered me with empty praise (the "kisses" of an enemy). Instead he chose the more difficult road of telling the truth, a painful but enriching experience for me. By pushing me to improve, he was looking out for my best interests in the long run. Not only did the writing improve, but the friendship grew even stronger. The wisdom writer explains, "As iron sharpens iron, so one man sharpens another" (Prov. 27:17).

Frederick Buechner says, "To speak the truth with love is to run the risk always of speaking only the truths that people love to hear you speak." You will probably have many pleasant but essentially shallow acquaintances in college. But superficial friends will not love you enough to take risks on your behalf or to administer the pain of the strike so as to wound and then comfort you in the healing. It seems that "good friends" are the tools with which God often chooses to sharpen our insights and abilities. We are improved under each other's care, refined through mutual trust. How can this happen? Why do we openly subject ourselves to the scalpel of a friend? Even if we do not recognize the need for surgery, we will invite the blade if we trust that the doctor is friendly and faithful to do all that needs to be done.

And so we come again to honesty. Wounds from enemies intend to harm, to accelerate a victim's movement toward death. In contrast, the injuries inflicted by true friends are meant to cut out the cancer of sin—or destroy the deadly virus of spiritual disease—and advance the movement toward life. One difference between the two approaches is that friends do not thrust the sword and then leave you for the vultures. Instead, they pierce no more than is necessary to extract or annihilate the accursed thing. Then friends bind up your wound and apply the soothing balm of understanding and loving advice. One is a destroyer; the other is a healer who will be faithful, who will come to comfort you, to see you through till you are better. Since your recovery may take considerable time—and we are in no better than a state of recovery all our lives—you will need steadfast friends, people who will stay by you through the tough times because they are being used by God on your behalf. As I said, these kindred spirits are rare. Yet Scripture encourages us to live in this kind of relationship: "He who walks with the wise grows wise, but a companion of fools suffers harm" (Prov. 13:20).

Courage and Faithfulness

Indeed, it is a privilege, one of the Father's many mercies, to be able to interact with joyful, intimate, and edifying soulmates. In the same teaching in which Jesus called his disciples "friends," he stated the highest standard of friendship: "Greater love has no one than this, that he lay down his life for his friends" (John 15:13). Having endured the most mortal of wounds for us, the Lord remains faithful to his friends, to everyone who has accepted his sacrificial gift. This kind of allegiance often requires brave and selfless commitment in times of serious testing. With our tendency to sneeze through relationships, we could use as many heroes as we can find to show us a vision of this Christlike loyalty.

History is full of famous romantic pairs: Cleopatra and Marc Antony, Napoleon and Josephine, Kermit and Miss Piggy. Perhaps because the love called "friendship" is thought to be less exciting than male-female "passion," we have few renowned same-gender duos to reflect upon. One biblical account of such a relationship involves Jonathan and David, recorded in 1 and 2 Samuel.

At this time in Israel's history, Saul was king, but he was neither a good leader nor a faithful man of God. After David slew Goliath with a stone and prayer, Saul brought the humble shepherd boy to court and commissioned him in the royal army. The people admired David, too, and Saul soon began to be angered by such backhanded compliments (more like nanny-goat insults) as "Saul has slain his thousands, and David his tens of thousands" (1 Sam. 18:7).

Not caring much for being upstaged by David, Saul decided to play darts with his protégé, using him for a board. All those years of dodging marauding beasts to protect the sheep paid off for David and he escaped.

Enter Jonathan, Saul's son and rightful heir to the throne. So "one in spirit with David" was Jonathan that they made a covenant with each other, pledging loyalty and deep friendship. As David's popularity and successes against the Philistines multiplied, Saul's anger grew and Jonathan's faithfulness was tested. Even though it would cost him his throne, Jonathan not only aided David but promoted his cause before the people. When Saul again attempted to murder David, Jonathan told his father, "Let not the king do wrong to his servant David; he has not wronged you, and what he has done has benefited you greatly" (1 Sam. 19:4). In other words, "What's he ever done to you, Dad?"

Later, with all the suspense of a modern-day spy thriller, Jonathan worked out a code to get a secret message to David, warning him whenever Saul concocted a new assassination plot. When they met in a field where David had been hiding, they realized that they would henceforth be separated, because David was a hunted man. The Scripture reads that they "wept together—but David wept the most. Jonathan said to David, 'Go in peace, for we have sworn friendship with each other in the name of the LORD . . .'" (1 Sam. 20:41–42).

The last time the two young men saw each other was during Saul's last gasp of tracking down David. In defiance of his father and therefore at great risk to his own life, Jonathan

went to David at Horesh and helped him find strength in God. "Don't be afraid," he said. "My father Saul will not lay a hand on you. You will be king over Israel, and I will be second to you. Even my father Saul knows this." The two of them made a covenant before the LORD . . . (1 Sam. 23:16–18).

Can you imagine the depth of encouragement this must have been for David? There he was: a fugitive, alienated from the king, compelled to feign insanity and eat holy bread just to stay alive. Then up trots the prince—his best friend and covenantal companion who had risked the wrath of his father—to tell him that he need not be frightened. What a blessing Jonathan's faithfulness must have been to David.

Here we have a model of courageous loyalty you are unlikely to see duplicated. You might well ask: "Who are the Jonathans in my life? In whose life am I a Jonathan?"

David never saw his friend again. In a fierce battle against the Philistines, both Saul and Jonathan died. At their funeral, David revealed his own remarkable character by speaking graciously about Saul, his oppressor, and affirming the measure of his commitment to Jonathan, his good and steadfast friend:

> Saul and Jonathan—
> in life they were loved and gracious,
> and in death they were not parted.
> They were swifter than eagles,
> they were stronger than lions. . . .
> How the mighty have fallen in battle!
> Jonathan lies slain on your heights.
> I grieve for you, Jonathan, my brother;
> you were very dear to me.
> Your love for me was wonderful,
> more wonderful than that of women.
>
> (2 Sam. 1:23, 25–26)

I am stunned by the courage of Jonathan. I am hushed by the nobility of David. Jonathan and David show us what friends can be to one another. May the Lord grace you with such a friend.

As you contemplate these heroes, note that Jonathan and David were not casual about their friendship. They made covenants. They were willing to be inconvenienced. They laughed and planned and took risks together. The fact that they *wept* together is ample proof of their common vision, their mutuality of interest, and their protectiveness of each other.

Can we develop Jonathan-and-David friendships in our transient culture? Yes, but not if we blindly follow the crowd by doing no more than going to movies together or chattering about the latest scandal. Sometimes we media-indoctrinated materialists are prone to neglect intangible and lasting values, in favor of money and possessions. Jesus said that "where your treasure is, there your heart will be also" (Matt. 6:21). Let us then value most highly the best of all possible gifts, our faithful friends, who are hard to find in a throwaway, plasticized society.

Your parents have probably been telling you for years that all your choices count, "but be especially careful how you choose your friends." Amen to that! My message here has been less obvious: Good friends are not necessarily an endangered species, but neither are they easy to identify. Covenantal companionships require *time*, the risk-taking that honesty implies, and the faithfulness of sacrifice. Since good friends usually don't stay close by forever, unless you preserve the connection in letters, calls, visits, and special arrangements to see each other, even an "undying friendship" will fade. The "aha" moments when you can say "You, too? I thought I was the only one . . ." are remarkable gifts from God to be cherished and protected. Few things this side of heaven can bring such joy.

What's in Your Heart?

1. What distinguishes your most enduring friendships from the ones that have faded after a few months?
2. How have you experienced "wounds from a friend can be trusted"?
3. What do you most admire about the friendship between Jonathan and David? To what ends have you gone to preserve what is best described as "the fellowship of kindred souls"?

9

Sex: It's Both Less and More Than You Think

Love's mysteries in souls do grow,
But yet the body is his book.
John Donne

What do political candidates, milk, cars, deodorant, and the new XT-5 Super Vise-Grip Pliers have in common? The answer is obvious: sex! We all know that sex is used to sell anything. When a scantily clad woman slinks along the length of a sports car, running her hand along the hood in a way that would give goose bumps to any red-blooded fender, we don't need to ask, "Does she come with the car?" We know that she does.

In many old movie Westerns, there is a scene in which a conniving huckster sweet-talks honest dollars out of hard-working,

115

God-fearing pioneers for a jar of fake medicine. This syrupy solution is offered as a cure-all for everything from headaches to heartaches. The salesman bellows, "Buy Dr. Jake's Miracle Tonic! It'll cure colds, flu, leprosy, acne, constipation, diarrhea, and hangnails—in fact, anything that ails you!" In our modern sophistication, we laugh, shake our heads, and think, "I can't believe people actually bought that stuff." But isn't sex hyped as a tonic for *our* age? Don't many of us believe the happy huckster who tells us that sex makes *everything* better?

Perhaps the next generation will laugh and shake their heads at our gullibility. For example, not only do we listen to Madonna's silly claim that we ought to vote because "freedom of speech is as good as sex," we spend considerable time and money filling our minds with the most incredible notions about sexuality. In one trip to a college bookstore newsstand, I noticed nine titles about sex on the covers of magazines (and these weren't pornographic publications). In *Self,* there was "International Sex: What They're Doing That We're Not." *Glamour* featured "Sex Debate on New Path to Orgasm"; *Psychology Today* told about "Transsexual Passages"; *Life* offered "Profile on *Playboy's* Christie Hefner." In movies, ads, and TV shows, the message about the miracle tonic is clear: Sex will cure whatever ails you.

Although AIDS, herpes, and other medical facts of life have made many Americans more cautious about sexual adventure, the college campus is typically the least restrained environment around. Granted, some of you will be on much less sexually permissive campuses. Even so, the college climate tends to encourage either sexual experimentation or sexual anxiety. What else would you expect when you move hormonally crazed and sexually stimulated *homo sapiens* away from protective homes and put them physically close to one another?

Before you begin to think that I recommend a segregated society where men and women never meet except to exchange fertilized test-tubes, I would direct your attention to a few questions. What do you think about sex? Is it something you ought to feel guilty about? Or is it something you should *never* feel guilty about? What would you say to a roommate who slept with someone after a party? What would you do if a romantic interest took an interest in exploring your body?

Debunking the Hype

As Christians, good thinking and good choices about sex are vital to your happiness and spiritual health. But, while some students treat sexual topics as "unmentionable," others loudly assert that as long as they are neither as stuffy as their ancestors nor as promiscuous as "pagans," any behavior is okay. In between the silence and the shouting, certain important questions are missed: What is a biblical view of sexuality? How does it relate to our times? Although the tonic you bought tastes delicious, is it all it's cracked up to be? Does it have dangerous side effects? In addressing these questions, an analysis of a few cultural messages may help you gain perspective.

Cultural Message #1: Romance Without Sex Is Like Dinner Without Dessert

Some people seem to regard sex about the same way they think about dessert. Depending on your view of dessert, you might regard romance without sex anywhere from a disappointment ("Oh, well, at least the main course was good") to a tragedy ("What a wasted evening. The only reason I put up with lima beans was for the cherry pie!"). For some, romance (whatever that means) is fulfilling only when it inevitably leads to sex. Since romance is supposedly what gives life "meaning," life without sex would be a contradiction in terms. Most movies, among other media, peddle this message with grand repetition. *Of course*, the hero and heroine will end up in bed. Can you imagine Harry telling Sally, "Naw, let's wait until we're married"?

Another part of this fanciful message is that sex adds magical wonder to any relationship. It brings us not merely physical pleasure, but that element we so long for in modern life: intimacy. On the one hand, this is true. Because sex is the most intimate physical act that can exist between two people, the participants often feel emotionally connected after a sexual encounter. *At least for a time.* On the other hand, physical intimacy does not guarantee emotional closeness. The sexual experience will not produce mutuality of concern, assure loyalty, or heal psychological problems. If that were the case, both prostitutes and their clients would be overwhelmed with a bounty of intimate and loving relationships. Contrary to the made-for-TV version, it just ain't so.

Sex may function as a dessert in some circumstances, but it's a mistake to believe it to be the treat that will make everything better. Yet this is a hard message to resist. Even though bitter experience shows us that sex can produce alienation as easily as intimacy, we still lust after the improbable events that blaze before us across a forty foot screen.

Cultural Message #2: Sex Is Like a Good Belch

Another common view is that sexual intercourse is a perfectly natural phenomenon that should no more be resisted than a rising bubble of gas in the throat. Other animals are not inhibited about natural acts like sex, so why should we be? Hugh Hefner and others have persuaded many that the simple pleasurable physiology of sex ("like a glass of fine wine") should not be restricted by two-bit moralizers.

The strength of the "good belch" theory rests in the intuitive appeal of certain data. The reasoning is that (1) sex is a physical act; (2) physical acts are natural; and (3) natural needs ought to be met. What would happen if you did not eat or drink or burp or cough? Pressure would build.

Chaos would reign. Deep, dark Freudian things would happen to your mind. You would become a hideous, unnatural, repressed creature. The implication is: You must join the wildest fraternity and sow your oats or you'll never get any grain.

The trouble with this theory (besides its crassness) is threefold. First, sex is not merely a physical act. It is deeply psychological (more on that later in this chapter). In fact, there is no such thing as a "purely physical" relationship. For all the hoopla about the casual simplicity of sex, virtually no one treats it that way. The Good Belchers want it badly, talk about it incessantly, look at pictures of it whenever possible. All this for a momentary burst of relief?

Second, all physical drives are not equally important for our survival. The sex drive is not the same as the hunger drive. Contrary to Hugh and his buddies, we can do without sex and be happy, healthy individuals. Not so with hunger. Giving birth is a "natural act," but should a woman get pregnant every time she longs for a baby? All natural urges must wait to be satisfied in an appropriate context (even hungry students must wait for their professor to stop yapping and let them go to lunch), but some drives are far more urgent than sex.

Third, sexual desire is not like burp-pressure, which, without release, will build and become increasing painful. The hucksters are lying. We don't need a frequent dose of sexual tonic to live well. We won't become ill if we don't perform regularly in bed. When sex is viewed as mere biology, there is often an overstated concern with technique. Books such as *Joy of Sex* and *More Joy of Sex* fit into this orientation. An older friend of mine ridicules this step-by-step approach, "The human race is thousands of years old, but *your* generation needs color-coded sex manuals." The focus of Good Belchers is not on the person but on the performance, an emphasis that de-personalizes the most personal human interaction.

How Sex Comes Down When It's Raised Up

Although many other messages about sex are present in our culture's dining room and especially in most college cafeterias, the Dessert Theory and the Belch Theory dominate the menu. Yet these two messages seem contradictory. How can sex be both an "ennobling culmination of romantic intimacy" and "a mere animalistic craving that must not be denied"? One outlook promotes sex as primarily an emotional high, and the other views it as physical tension that demands release. Can sexual activity really deliver on both of these claims?

These two views do hold some things in common. Both glorify sex by making extravagant claims about it. The Dessert Lovers claim that only sex can express the magnitude of feeling in a relationship. The Good Belchers insist that the physical pleasure of sex is the summit of human experience. With the help of the media, both camps so expansively tout their views that you would have to live a hermit's life to avoid eight zillion messages a year extolling the virtues of sex. On daytime soap operas, for example, 90 percent of all sexual encounters are between unmarried partners. I grieve for women like the high school girl who told me, "I've been having sex with a boy I don't even like anymore. I want to stop but peer pressure is *so* hard to resist." Wouldn't "obsession" be a good word for society's attitude toward sex?

Ironically, the more that sex has been glorified in our culture, the more it has also been debased. Sexual behavior has become so common that it seems to be divorced not only from marriage and procreation, but from love or even ordinary affection. George Leonard, once a promoter of the Sexual Revolution of the 60s, has recently noticed what he calls "the end of sex":

> Something strange has happened to sex in our time. . . . You can read scores of current sex books and not once come across the word love. And, paradoxically, leading sexologists,

while insisting that sex be viewed as a natural function integral to daily life, seem to want to remove it from social and ethical considerations. This removal fosters the notion that our erotic behavior actually has little or nothing to do with anything else in our lives and thus is essentially trivial.

The trouble with sex today is that it is pursued for its own sake, to achieve a momentary exotic feeling of intimacy or an erotic sensation of *physical* pleasure. Sex has thereby become debased, trivialized, cheapened.

We can conclude from the analysis that sex is *less* than we think. It is not a cure-all tonic, not the answer to all of our physical and emotional needs. Sex is not the source of soul-satisfying intimacy, nor will it be truly gratifying if pursued obsessively in a search for continual ecstasy. Commenting about the limits of pornography, a man once said, "What you see is what you get."

Sexual expression cannot create intimacy from physical sensation alone. It is equally limited in the minutes of pleasure it can provide in any given day. Since sex ultimately fails to deliver on its overstated claims, disillusioned Dessert Lovers eventually tend to become members of the Lonely Hearts Club, wondering how their promiscuity led them astray. On the other hand, Good Belchers begin as party-people and tend to become lechers, compulsively seeking more and more pleasure at others' expense. When the importance of sex is exaggerated, others are exploited for the gratifier's gain, being "used" for pleasure or manipulated into making a meaningless commitment. Sex is not a good master, because it was never meant to have so much power over human behavior. *Sex is less than we think.*

But sex is also *more* than we usually think, and here lies a great paradox. Though our culture glorifies sex when it should be treated more humbly, it also degrades sex when it should be honored and protected. Because we overstate its potential to fulfill our lives and understate its intended purpose, we do not protect ourselves and others from sexual abuse.

The Purpose of Sex or "The Song of Songs" Says *What?*

One of the most negative and *incorrect* images of God is that of Celestial Scrooge, an old fuddy-duddy who can't bear to see anyone having a good time. This view, which is tragic theology, comes more from our own sense of guilt than it does from the Scriptures. James reminds us that each "good and perfect gift is from above, coming down from the Father of the heavenly lights . . ." (1:17). God is the Author of every pleasure; all evil is merely a perversion of his original intent.

We don't have to go far in the Bible to see this quality of God at work. Genesis 1 tells us how he created the world and called it good, which implies something about his sense of enjoyment. Then, in Genesis 2, the first reference to human sexuality is recorded: "For this reason, a man will leave his father and mother and be united to his wife, and they will become one flesh" (v. 24).

This statement is worth a little investigation. Genesis 2 tells us a lot about Adam, including his loneliness, his need for a suitable companion. After everything else that had been created to that point was found wanting in this respect (how long can you talk to an anteater?), God solved the problem by creating a woman, someone qualified to meet Adam on his own terms. But what was the "reason" that man and woman became one flesh? Once the search for a suitable ally was over and the answer to Adam's restlessness was provided, God's plan was revealed in full. That man and woman come together in commitment to each other is both appropriate and intended by the Creator. Men and women were designed as partners—meant to be married.

Walter Trobisch says in *I Married You* that the three verbal phrases in the verse—to *leave,* to *cleave* (KJV), and to *become one flesh*—also inform us about that relationship. To *leave* means to realign one's loyalties, to switch one's *primary* commitment from parents or other loved ones to each other. When a man and a woman marry, they are declaring that their former relationships and objects of dependence (whatever they were) will be rearranged and re-prioritized. The "leaving" symbolized by the wedding ceremony is not an abandonment of all other personal commitments, but testimony to a switch in primary loyalties.

To *cleave* means, literally, to stick to, to be glued to, to be united with. "Cleaving" is about accepting a new predominant commitment: spousal loyalty. It is to say that the beloved will be honored above all others, that one's spouse is to be the most important, most esteemed, and most significant influence in one's life. An image of two pieces of paper being glued together provides a strong analogy. The two pieces cannot be separated without causing significant damage to each piece. Whereas leaving is symbolized by the wedding ceremony, cleaving is represented by the vows themselves. The promise of fidelity "till death do us part" is a declaration about the durability of the glue, the lasting bond of commitment.

The third element in the verse is *become one flesh*. Since the phrase captures the various ways in which two individuals merge into a new entity, I like to call it "weaving." (Besides, it rhymes with "leaving" and "cleaving.") The weaving is to take place physically (the statement precedes the events of the Fall, so sex is not by definition sinful), but also economically, psychologically, and socially. To weave is to form a new life together, to act in society as "wed" to each other. Marriage is not about two individuals who lead essentially separate lives except for rooming together for convenience or sexual gratification. Marriage is about two people learning to function as one unit. Wendell Berry says, "To them, 'mine' is not so powerful or necessary a pronoun as 'ours.'"

Without losing their individuality, married "weavers" move from their adolescent lust for autonomous independence, not to absolute dependence, but to *inter*-dependence and cooperation. Jesus adds to the Genesis passage, "So they are no longer two, but one. Therefore what God has joined together, let man not separate" (Matt. 19:6). Weaving is symbolized by sexual intercourse. The physical union is evidence of an expression of, and contributes to the mystery of being "one flesh."

We can conclude that the purpose of sex is to foster the lover/beloved union found in marriage. In that setting, God intended sex to be a wonderful, pleasurable experience. Though Solomon's Song of Songs makes some churchgoers blush, there is ample proof in the sensual language of this love poetry that sexual intercourse is an appropriate way for two people to express their deep affection, loyalty, and mutuality. Here's one example (Song of Songs 4:5): "Your two breasts are like two fawns, like twin fawns of a gazelle that browse among the lilies" (let's assume it's a compliment). And so it also makes sense that, according to the Bible sexual intercourse can only "weave" honorably in the context of marriage.

The Nature of Sex or "Why Does It Say 'Adam Knew Eve'?"

Why all this talk about marriage in a book addressed to single college students? Among other things, your life in college will establish the patterns you will take with you into the rest of adulthood. The decisions you make won't belong only to these "carefree years"; they will also shape who you are and the nature of your future commitments. Sex is intended to be an expression of lifelong commitment. There's a great deal missing when it takes the form of that collegiate favorite: a one-night stand. But this gets us into the *nature* of the sex act.

If the purpose of our sexuality is to foster the love/beloved union, what is it about sexual behavior that accomplishes that goal? The mere fact that sex is pleasurable does not achieve that end, otherwise tandem surfing or reading a good book together would also be expressions of "weaving." Sexual union is meant to symbolize "one-fleshness" because it is the most significant sharing of intimate knowledge that can take place on the physical level.

The Bible frequently refers to sex in terms of "knowing" another person. The Bible does not say that Adam "knew" Eve because it is ashamed to use more direct terms. As the Song of Songs indicates ("your lips drop sweetness as the honeycomb, my bride," 4:11), the Bible is perhaps the earthiest of holy books. Instead, this terminology captures the idea that sex is *more* than we think. Sex is not a casual act, but the most significant *psychological* experience in which we can participate with another human being. The unmatchable glory of marital sex is that each partner has reserved this physical and emotional bonding for the spouse alone. The act of intercourse is then the most tangible way of telling the beloved that he or she is the very special someone to whom you want to be totally joined. It says, "Because you are the most important person in my world, I am sharing not only the most intimate part of myself, but a gift I have decided to offer to you alone."

Sex is unlike other human behavior in that when we have a sexual encounter of any kind, the psychological imprint will remain long after the physical sensation has passed. Can you not easily recall each sexually charged experience you have had? Haven't sexual situations touched you more deeply, even when involving a person for whom you did not care much, than experiences of less physical intimacy? The closer you have come to intercourse, the more likely this is true.

In *The Mystery of Marriage,* Mike Mason explains:

> Exposure of the body in a personal encounter is like the telling of one's deepest secret: afterwards there is no going back, no pretending that the secret is still one's own or that

the other does not know. It is, in effect, the very last step in human relations, and therefore never one to be taken lightly. . . . As a gesture symbolic of perfect trust and surrender, it requires the security of the most perfect of reassurances and commitments into which two people can enter, which is no other than the loving contract of marriage.

The consequences of this aspect of sex are significant. If sex is only a casual event that leaves no mark, what does it matter if we do it outside of marriage? If sex is a deeply pleasurable act that can be walked away from with little effect on us, why not try to get intimate as often as we see fit? But Scripture implies that sex leaves such a strong imprint on our total experience that to engage in it outside of the marital union is a tragedy that may affect our lives as dramatically as any other single act.

The kind of "knowledge" that is shared during sexual intercourse goes so deep that to transgress the marital context is to risk long-term, if not lifelong, damage. When asked in a recent sociological survey to list their most profound regret, a majority of respondents said "a poor decision about sex." If sex is so inconsequential, why can it have so many *bad* consequences? Why does a single childhood act of sexual abuse usually traumatize a woman for years, even for most of her adult life? If sex has no meaning except as an act of physical pleasure, why does Jesus say that the only reasonable cause for divorce is adultery? Is he not saying that the transgression from which a marriage will least likely recover is the sharing of physical intimacy with someone besides one's spouse?

Although repeated transgressions may cloud our understanding of the true nature of the sexual act (the way a con-artist views the next scam or an assassin treats murder), the apostle Paul reminds us: "Do you not know that he who unites himself with a prostitute is one with her in body?" (1 Cor. 6:16a). Something is going on here besides a good belch!

The Case Against Nonmarital Sex or "The Difference Between Tigers and Kitties"

Sex is a powerful tiger that needs a strong cage, not a friendly house cat that can come and go as it pleases. Of course, a tiger is such a beautiful and exciting beast that you may not be convinced about the need to limit its freedom; you'd rather take your chances with it in the wild.

That brings us to the topic of sex between unmarried partners, whether premarital or extramarital. You have probably deduced two things from the discussion so far. First, since sex should take place only within the context of marriage, nonmarital sex (what the Bible calls fornication) is immoral, inadvisable, and most likely regrettable, even though it may give pleasure at the moment. Second, since sex is an expression of total commitment, any sexual activity outside of marriage is a lie. Both of these ideas affirm what the Bible makes clear, that we "should avoid sexual immorality" and "learn to control" our own body (1 Thess. 4:3).

Before taking a closer look at the first point, I'd like to address the second. Why is all "nonmarital or unnatural sex" (the literal translation of the word *porneia* in the passage cited) a lie? If sex is meant to be unique knowledge that is exclusively reserved for my spouse, every time I share that knowledge with someone else, I am lying. I am refuting my vow to restrict this gift to my spouse. I am lying by acting as if what I promised would be unique to one relationship is actually something that I intended to share on some level with others.

If we try to relate the intense pleasure of sexual experience to the first point—the idea that nonmarital sex is immoral—the tendency is to wonder, "Why is God trying to ruin all my fun?" But he's not! Life would be so much simpler if doing good was always perfectly pleasurable and doing evil was vile and disgusting. Instead, sometimes doing the right thing means suffering and doing the wrong thing is enjoyable, at least in the short run. We can delight in all sorts of terrible things ranging from a sarcastic, biting remark (which someone "deserved"), to robbery, adultery, or even murder. Premarital sex can be an enjoyable experience. But enjoying it does not make it "right" or in our best interests. Why is it that sexual abstinence outside of marriage is God's design?

Because of the nature of sex. As already noted, sex is a unique bonding experience. In some mysterious way, two people tend to feel more unified after sex—they have become one flesh. But, because sex is a life-uniting act, it requires the life-united commitment of marriage. Sex, the physical expression of "becoming one flesh," is not only a symbol of oneness, it *is* a oneness. And the sexual drive, like other desires, grows more insistent when it is indulged. The more you accentuate sex in your lifestyle, the more you want it. Common collegiate fiction includes "just this once and then I'll be satisfied" or "I have this incredible need that will scar me for life if I don't fulfill it." Sexual desire is not satisfied that easily. One act leads to another with increasing ease. Saying "yes" increases the odds of saying "yes" next time. This is fine in marriage, although self-control is required in marriage, too. Outside of marriage, saying "yes" makes the temptation stronger. A college friend of mine once confided in me about his sexual struggles. He said that he envied virgins because he thought that his indulgence had made sexual discipline more difficult. There is a kind of "slippery slope" of sexual behavior.

Because of the nature of marriage. The Scriptures hold up marriage as a high estate, and sex within marriage is likewise praised. Marriage provides the foundation of trust that gives sex the security it needs to be fulfilling for both partners. One could compare sex to nitroglycerin, that volatile chemical that is safe if not jolted, but explodes when disturbed. In a solid marriage, the environment is stable enough to contain the volatile stuff of sex without mishap. Outside of marriage, things are so shaky that the resulting sexual explosion can hurl scar-producing shrapnel in all directions. Far from "spoiling our fun," God restricts sex to marriage for our physical and emotional protection.

"Living together" provides neither the security necessary for meaningful sex nor an adequate test of compatibility. How can a couple possibly "try on" or rehearse a lifelong partnership?

In marriages that have the confidence of longevity, unlike premarital relationships, one partner is unlikely to worry about the fickleness of the other, or be manipulated into sex against his or her wishes, or be caught up in an extramarital passion that would be regretted later. Also, though you'd never know it by the way sex is treated in movies or soap operas, sex and procreation actually have something to do with each other! Babies—those funny little gurgly, poopy blobs—more often result from sexual intercourse than any other leading brand of fun. In marriage, this is usually a joyous event. Outside of marriage, it is usually a tragedy for parent, child, or both.

Because of the nature of nonmarital relationships. There are many reasons to develop nonmarital platonic relationships. Surely, we are allowed to relate to the opposite sex in ways other than as potential romantic, sexual, or marital partners! Yet, considering the way many men and women treat each other, one might think that cross-gender friendships were impossible.

But what happens to a nonmarital relationship that becomes sexually oriented? Among other things, certain established behavior patterns tend to get carried over into marriage. For example, those who have premarital sex may feel guilty about it and continue to feel guilty about their sexuality after marriage. Or they may come to think that sex is only enjoyable when the rules are broken. Or that sex is justified in the heat of passion, that "being in love" sanctions unrestricted sexual expression. What would this mean for this person's potential for having an affair?

Prior sexual experience does not necessarily make a person a better married lover. If anything, the opposite may be the case. Some will learn to associate guilt or fear with sex. Others discover that they can only relate to their partner as a sex object, as someone to possess or conquer. And this is perhaps the most important issue here. How do we treat each other? Dallas Willard, in *The Spirit of the Disciplines*, has said that sexual self-control, or chastity, is the discipline that enables us to treat the opposite gender as fully human.

Paradoxically, chastity—the commitment to avoid sexual encounters with anyone except one's spouse—is a *freeing* experience. When you can see members of the opposite sex as something besides sexual outlets, you can stop trying to impress them and worrying whether they find you sexually attractive. Instead, you feel free to treat them as persons, fellow members of God's family—indeed, as Paul says, as "sisters" [or "brothers," as the case may be] (1 Tim. 5:2). Chastity does not mean *non*-sexuality, but *right-minded* sexuality. As Willard says, "Healthy abstention in chastity can only be supported by loving, positive involvement with members of the opposite sex . . . underscored with compassion, association and helpfulness. . . . To practice chastity, then, we must first practice love."

Taming the Beast

Inevitably, the idea of chastity leads to the oft-asked question, "Well, how far *can* I go?" In the Sermon on the Mount, Jesus said, "You have heard that it was said, 'Do not commit adultery.' But I tell you that anyone who looks at a woman lustfully has already committed adultery with her in his heart" (Matt. 5:27–28). After I get over my guilty depression from reading that passage, I find that it reconciles what I understand to be the nature of sex with the biblical prohibitions against sexual immorality.

What is sexual sin? It is trying to create a sexual reality that is other than what God intends. The action may be in your mind or between the sheets, but in either case it is a rejection of God's will regarding sex.

How does this resolve the question of how far is *too* far? Jesus is saying that we are not even to set the stage for nonmarital sexual intercourse. That's it. As any married couple will tell you, intercourse is not just the "penetration." It includes all the preliminary activity, including the involvement of the mind. Therefore, the only place to draw the line is at the very beginning. Is it any wonder that those couples who try to stop somewhere in the middle of the sex act are frustrated at not being able to finish? It's like telling someone to diet by chewing the chocolate and then spitting it out. As John White sagely puts it in *Eros Defiled:*

> How does one distinguish between petting and intercourse? Once you try to map out morality in terms of anatomy and physiology, you wind up with an ethical labyrinth from which there is no exit. . . . [I]s there any moral difference between two naked people in bed petting to orgasm and another two having intercourse? A look can be as sensual as a touch and a finger brushed lightly over a cheek as erotic as a penetration.

In other words, to answer the question, "How far can I go?" you must recognize when you actually *begin* sexual intercourse. When do you become "ready" to go? The answer is highly individual and also varies according to circumstance. If you're concerned about maintaining sexual purity, you need to be aware of your own desires and your sense of control. In some situations, you might be able to sustain a long embrace and not be sexually charged. At other times, you need to be careful how you even look at someone. You also always need to consider the purity of your partner. What you can enjoy without lust, others cannot. A man's tolerance of frustration is usually less than a woman's, and men will often push whatever limits have been set (sometimes they'll just push!). Nevertheless, straightforward sexual activity should be out of the question in any nonmarital situation. As Solomon put it, "Do not arouse or awaken love until it so desires" (Song of Songs 2:7).

Another way to look at chastity is to suggest that you should behave like a married person would legitimately behave toward someone besides his or her spouse. As a married man intent on staying "cleaved" to my wife, extramarital sex is simply not an option for me. I must be on my guard when I am with someone whom I find attractive, usually by avoiding any physical contact whatsoever. With others, I might feel free to give them a hug. This analogy breaks down eventually, since for me no other woman is a marital option but for single persons the next relationship may lead to wedding cake. Because most "next relationships" do not, the comparison still has validity.

When I come to this point in the material, I feel a bit like the dad who has bundled up his child in so many sweaters and coats that the poor kid can barely move. Then he says, "Go outside now and have fun." There are many important issues remaining, including the specifics of dealing with sexual guilt and learning to exercise sexual control. Since there are many other places to find help with these concerns, suffice it to say here that, though the scars from sexual immorality heal slowly, sexual sins can be easier to admit than other sins. The Old and New Testaments offer the reassurance that God's grace and understanding have been extended to sexual stumblers since the earliest of times.

One possible response to the biblical view of sexuality is to regard it as hopelessly out of date, cruel, ridiculous, and unachievable on any college campus in modern America. Perhaps so, but let's look at the supporting evidence: (1) the sex act is a profound experience, with enormous potential for abuse; (2) the marital union provides the most secure environment for a healthy expression of sex; (3) the Bible is clear about the need to take sexual sin seriously. As preposterous as it may sound in our sexually saturated culture, premarital chastity and fidelity in marriage represent the wisest and most godly ways to fulfill the Creator's purpose for our sexuality.

Because sex is *less* than we think, we ought not overstate its riches or put too much hope it it. But, because sex is also *more* than we think, we ought to protect it, recognize the massive risks we take when we toy with it, and "love our neighbors" without treating them as sexual objects.

What's in Your Heart?

1. In your own words, explain how sex is both less and more than we think.
2. Which "cultural message" about sex is most attractive to you? How do you combat it? How do you feed it?
3. Discuss a recent, popular, romantic movie. What did the movie assume about the role of sex in relationships? What do you agree with or disagree with?

Is Dating Emotional Fornication?

In holy things may be unholy greed.

George MacDonald

You've seen it all before: Boy meets girl, boy and girl flirt, boy and girl fall head-over-shoes in love, boy and girl disrobe for an evening of wrestling and groaning, boy and girl break up. And that's usually just the first twenty-four hours.

Okay, maybe that hasn't actually happened to you, but all of us have experienced that story line *vicariously* dozens of times or more. Every Friday night, millions of single Americans crowd the movie theaters and live out their romantic/sexual fantasies by observing the action on the screen. Many in the audience leave the theater yearning for intimacy (or at least the back seat) and, in effect, say to their date, "Let's go out and try what we just saw," or perhaps, "If only *you* could be like that!"

135

The pattern unfolds with unceasing predictability, partly because a movie or TV drama with the title *The Restrained Adventures of Temperate Tommy and Disciplined Diane* wouldn't attract much of a following. The silliness of the title is instructive. Among other reasons, the concept is ridiculous because we have been programmed to know what is *supposed* to happen when boy meets girl and don't really want to hear otherwise. (One wonders if romance had more variety before the advent of movies.)

Apart from the influence of the media and the need for discernment, the pertinent issues here are the nature of the American version of romance and your involvement with it while in college. What do you believe about dating? With so many campus-wide prospects for affection, this aspect of wooing the opposite sex seems an appropriate topic. Besides causing the everyday sorts of relational traumas that go with being at a coeducational institution, the college experience has an uncanny way of keeping the marriage chapel pretty busy after graduation.

Dating American-Style (or How to *Think* You're Having More Fun Than You're Having)

Most people spend many hours agonizing over decisions to be made in various romantic relationships before committing to a one-and-only partner. Yet, typically we spend little time evaluating our culture's assumptions about the dating-to-marriage ritual that seems as natural and inevitable as breakfast in the morning. But, just as eggs and bacon have been discovered to be a less-than-healthy way to begin the day, the American pattern of matchmaking has its own kind of social cholesterol. Four characteristics of the contemporary dating scene are worth examining.

First, dating tends to be *exclusive*. Even on the first outing, a dating duo is referred to as a twosome, a distinctive unit that precludes other attachments. One expectation in dating is to take the vague idea of pairing off and refine it into a specific, identifiable claim: "We are a *Couple*." The boy-meets-girl phenomenon often leads to some measure of commitment, which grants to each person certain rights and privileges, at least until they break up. At the Altar of Going Steady, the pair will vow "till somebody better comes along do us part."

Second, dating is about *romance,* a storybook concept dependent on "falling in love"—preferably in idyllic terms, complete with the blushing glance, the rush of the first touch, and an obsession with the beloved. One could say that the primary purpose of dating is to have romantic fun. Each time you go out, especially with someone new, you have high expectations that here is your big chance to find romance—affection, understanding, excitement, or whatever you think you've been missing so far. In fact, you have sweaty palms and lose your ability to speak coherently because you keep hearing the internal question, "Does he [she] like me?" Even if you just met, even if you don't like each other and there is a spoken or unspoken agreement that continuing the relationship is out of the question, both of you persist in acting "like a date" when on a date. The romantic tenor of dating, irrespective of commitment, is so ingrained that when Mom begins to worry about "Hannah's dreamy eyes," daughter snaps back, "Relax. I'm not going to marry him!" Silly Mom, dating is about swooning and crooning, not about *marriage.*

Third, dating pushes a couple toward *privacy.* Sooner or later the smitten love birds will tire of meeting in the noisy Student Union, with all its distractions. How can they coo and "get to know each other" unless they find an aviary all to themselves? By definition, dating is about being "a couple," and being a couple requires intimacy, and intimacy requires seclusion. End of discussion. Please close the door on the way out so that we can be alone.

Fourth, dating encourages *sexual activity.* When blankets of "romantic" devotion and downy pillows of love language are expressed in private (see above), sexual intimacy seems to want to, well, hop right in bed too. The expectation in the American dating scene is that the physical expression of love gradually increases as dating becomes more "serious." Of course sometimes the expectations do not wait for any sort of commitment. Men often expect women to "put out" after a certain amount of time or money has been spent on them. One of my friends in high school declared that if a girl was not sitting "thigh against thigh" with him by the time they left her driveway, he would turn around and drop her off. (An idle boast, I'm sure, but at least his heart was in the wrong place.) Women may not expect their dates to "put out," but without some show of physical affection a woman may doubt her partner's commitment or her own desirability.

"You Belong to *Me!*"

What conclusions derive from this analysis? I have come to think that the American version of boyfriend/girlfriend usually leads to a quasi-marital state that could be called "emotional fornication."* As recounted in the previous chapter, the biblical mandate about sex is clear but difficult: *The privilege of sex requires the lifetime commitment of marriage.* Might there be some other aspect of relations that requires the commitment of marriage? I believe so. Just as *physical* union is meant to be delayed until marriage, *emotional* "weaving" with another person (see chapter 9) should not be consummated until that time.

"Emotional fornication" refers to the premature expression of loyalty to one another. Like physical fornication, it attempts to live out one of the privileges of marriage without the responsibility of making a lifelong pledge. After having made death-do-us-part promises on their wedding day, the bride and groom now have heavenly permission to be

*I would like to thank Jack Crabtree for coining that phrase.

responsible to each other. The biblical directive is "do not act united until you are formally united." The dangers of premature commitment, like those of premarital sex, stem from snatching a gift of God out of its proper context. The quasi-marital status that "going steady" amounts to is simply a counterfeit version of the marital state that is not meant to have God's blessing. Elisabeth Elliot explains this situation in *Passion and Purity:*

> Unless a man is prepared to ask a woman to be his wife, what right has he to claim her exclusive attention? Unless she has been asked to marry him, why would a sensible woman promise any man her exclusive attention? If, when the time has come for a commitment, he is not man enough to ask her to marry him, she should give him no reason to presume that she belongs to him.

The kind of exaggerated possessiveness that marks most "seriously dating" couples is a distortion of the principle that *married* people have a right to demand faithfulness from their partner, that a certain amount of jealousy is appropriate, and that spouses are accountable to each other for their time, among other things. As dating becomes exclusive, many feel they have the right to say, "Mine! Hands off!"

The following exchange might take place on any given night on any given campus in America:

> "So where were *you* last night?" inquires Ross.
> "I went to a movie with some friends," responds Erin. "Is that so terrible?"
> "Which friends—male or female?" asks Ross. "I've got a right to know. I mean, haven't we made a commitment to one another?"
> Realizing her transgression, Erin admits, "You're right. I should have told you my plans."

Although the above conversation sounds innocent enough, the assumptions (and jealousy) behind Ross's cross-examination are justifiable only in the case of married couples. Sometimes individuals make life-changing decisions (such as refusing a job or transferring to another college) simply to meet the demands of loyalty in a dating relationship. If the couple chooses not to marry, each individual still must live with the practical consequences of those choices.

Dating is emotional fornication if the couple attempts to live as if they have already taken the vows of marriage. The privilege of "holy jealousy"—the right to have the other account for certain decisions and the claim to exclusive attention—is part of the experience of being married. It reflects part of what the Bible calls being "one flesh," for there are many "unions" that marriage implies. For example, on our wedding day, my wife and I vowed to be intertwined not only physically, but also psychologically, economically, and emotionally. To be "one flesh" is to live together before God and the world as a unit, no longer "Greg" or "Janet" (or even "Greg *and* Janet") but "the Spencers." Since we have undertaken to function in society as a kind of single organism (not that we do this admirably all the time), it is entirely appropriate that we know each other's plans and see ourselves as caught up together in the privilege, responsibility, and mystery of our union.

Of course, because we are still unique and sinful *individuals,* we have the potential to abuse these privileges. Sex could be abused in adultery or manipulation. Loyalty could be abused in extramarital commitments ("emotional adultery"?) or in the creation of an oppressive, confining atmosphere in the home. Even so, the promise of exclusivity and total fidelity is only proper in the context of marriage. In a Christian marriage, each partner belongs to the other, second only to his or her commitment to God.

In marriage, the task of honorable accountability is difficult enough. In dating, since the strings of "going steady" are never strong enough to bear the weight of such loyalty, this holy jealousy nearly always deteriorates into possessiveness. The critical determinant seems to be that if an experience is at the heart of marital "privilege," the experiences should wait until after the wedding. There are many ways to cheat the union of being one flesh. For example, does "going steady" warrant partial sexual intimacy? Contrary to popular practice, the Scriptures teach otherwise. Outside the protection of marriage, the responsibilities of sexual expression and its consequences—including the vulnerability to emotional pain and the need to honor the declaration "I give you my all"—are virtually ignored. Likewise, the responsibilities of loyalty are not protected outside of marriage: the preparation to bear one another up in sickness, frailty, depression, and so on. To modify a recent advertising slogan: "We should call no one 'mine' before it's time."

Yet it is also hard to wait if "everyone else" seems less patient, especially around January of your senior year when Engagement-O-Rama strikes. The older you get, the greater will be the pressure to "have a steady." But, as in all moral dilemmas, the primary issue is one's faith. Why wait for a vow of loyalty? Why sacrifice today's joy for tomorrow's promise? *Because you trust God.* You trust that he knows better than you do, that he has your best interests in mind, that, in fact, *his* ways are ultimately more pleasureable and less painful than your own.

So What Does Confirmed Bachelor St. Paul Know about Dating?

Unfortunately, the Bible does not have a special section on dating (or on such other contemporary issues as TV, nuclear weapons, and birth control). But there *are* many texts that discuss relationships. Two especially sound ones come from the pen of the apostle Paul: Romans 14 and 1 Corinthians 7.

In the Romans 14 passage, Paul comments on the specifics of minor doctrinal squabbles and then lists a guiding principle or two for our dealings with other people. He argues that since we do not live to please ourselves but the Lord (vv. 7–8), our behavior should strive for what is found in his kingdom: righteousness and peace and joy (v. 17). Specifically, we should "do what leads to peace and to mutual edification" (v. 19). Sound advice for any interpersonal situations including opposite-sex relationships. A related question might be, "Does dating encourage peace, harmony, joy, righteousness, mutual improvement—and all other noble qualities?" What has been your experience?

When Paul directs his teaching toward singleness in 1 Corinthians 7, he suggests that the unmarried state has at least two advantages over being married: less divided devotion to God (vv. 32, 34) and fewer troubles from societal and family pressures (vv. 28, 33). Paul believes that the single-minded pursuit of the Lord is easier for the single person not distracted by the responsibilities of marriage. If this is true, for single people to act *as if* they were married would be the worst of both worlds. The advantages of singleness would be lost without gaining the advantages of marriage.

Two principles, then, are pertinent to followers of Christ who are not yet married: (1) you should encourage the pursuit of peace and mutual edification in all your relationships, and (2) you should take advantage of your single state as a way to avoid entanglements that could draw your attention away from the discipleship to which every Christian is called.

Given these principles, premarital possessiveness (what I've been calling emotional fornication) does not measure up very well. First, dating one person exclusively is often not peaceful. Many conflicts erupt over what freedoms are permitted or denied. Jealousy, too, causes conflict, as do the decisions one has to make so as to honor whatever promises have been exchanged. Second, sexual expectations rarely lead to "mutual edification," let alone harmony. The Battle of the Blouse is waged often, and when it ends in unconditional surrender, both combatants have ceased to ask what is good for the other. Third, the emotional upheaval caused by successive infatuations and breakups "disrupts the peace," and it can acclimate you to the idea that canceling a commitment is an acceptable way to resolve conflict. Aren't you then learning patterns that make you more comfortable with divorce? Fourth, the state of steady dating inhibits the freedom that is the blessing of singleness, yet cheats you of the comforting security that is wedlock's glory. Since most young people are usually either "on the make" or with one word could become "on the make," they live in fear of not being attached or of becoming unattached. God's designs for singleness and marriage are meant to be free from these fears.

In light of Paul's standards, American-style dating practices do not appear to be conducive to relational or moral health. Even so-called innocent or casual dating can be destructive because it assumes the legitimacy of common romantic standards. As you examine your own experience, do the problems inherent in emotional fornication ring true?

If you're still with me, you may be wondering if I remember what it was like to be a Christian single, possibly lonely and confused about how to relate to the opposite sex without coming across as that none-too-rare species, the Tongue-tied Red-faced Footswallower. Yes, I do remember all that—but I have also since learned that there is a better way to journey toward each other than to head off down the dating path, hand-in-hand with the first dashing or compatible person around. Although there's a slight chance you might avoid the poison oak and thistles and make it to the right camp site, you may also suffer deep scrapes and ugly bruises. Sometimes the "better way" requires you to backtrack and try a new path altogether.

In the Beginning, Friendship

What I'm suggesting is that you replace the cycle of Dating/Engagement/Marriage with Friendship/Courtship/Marriage. We have seen that whenever "dating" essentially means "mating," its rituals and rules run counter to Paul's call for "peace and mutual edification." Yet, despite what your raging hormones, the media, and some of your peers are telling you, Paul's lofty goals are within your reach—especially if your heterosexual relationships begin as *friendships* and continue on that basis until there is joint agreement that marriage is a distinct possibility.

The American version of dating as summarized by the four characteristics we've been discussing, is diametrically opposed to the make-friends-first axiom. First, whereas dating tends to be exclusive, friendship is inclusive and open-ended. Three friends are better than two, and four better than three, as long as the newcomers mesh with the orientation and personalities of the old group. Second, dating is seclusive and seeks privacy. For friends, however, solitude is not advantageous except when discussing confidential or sensitive subject matter. Third, as they participate in public, socially-oriented experiences, heterosexual friends can relate interpersonally yet avoid dating's romantic orientation. C. S. Lewis said in *The Four Loves,* "Lovers are normally face to face, absorbed in each other; friends, side by side, absorbed in some common interest." Fourth, whereas dating raises expectations of physical response (no matter how "spiritual" the two people think they are), friendship arouses only such personal expectations as trustworthiness and sympathy.

A man and woman who simply want to get to know each other do not strive for exclusiveness, privacy, or romance. In fact, their focus is usually not on the relationship but on the commonality that binds them. Does this mean that a man and a woman should never go together to a movie and for coffee afterward? It depends. The most helpful way to distinguish between dating and friendship is not to make a legalistic list of things one can and cannot do, but to work at answering the question: "What do same-sex friends do?" If they treat each other the way you are treating your opposite-sex friend, you can be more confident that you are not slipping into emotional fornication. Perhaps Paul had this relational style in mind when he wrote about treating "younger women as sisters, with absolute purity" (1 Tim. 5:2).

Some things are rather clearly defined, however. Do friends hold hands? Do friends "make out" on the couch? Does George get mad when Bob visits Sam? Not in most normal same-sex friendships. But do friends go to movies? Do friends go out for coffee or a sandwich together? Do friends have some measure of commitment to each other? Of course they do. *Friends* don't stare into each other's eyes, or talk a lot about their relationship, or worry about whether it's okay for Teresa to have a conversation with Steve's roommate in plain sight of everyone. But whether the friends are named "George and Bob" or "Teresa and Steve," they can care deeply about each other. True friendships share a sense of loyalty that never deteriorates into "I belong to you" possessiveness.

In addition, because friendship is not *expected* to lead to romance, the pain, regret, and destructive patterns of "going steady" and "breaking up" can be sidestepped. Many men and women never think of relating to the opposite sex except as potential romantic or sexual partners. Think of the joy that is missed when half of the human race is eliminated as a source of companionship and emotional support!

Of course, given the mysteries of person-to-person attraction and our culture's preoccupation with sensuality and instant gratification, a commitment to platonic friendship swims against the prevailing current. Those who decide to follow this path may find that it is preferable to stick to group activities and avoid situations which are not stereotypical dating events. Special interest campus clubs, such as Habitat for Humanity, University Singers, or InterVarsity Christian Fellowship, provide an alternative focus.

Does this mean that those who choose to explore friendship first will not later become infatuated and want "something more" from the relationship? No. That's the hardest part. That powerful sense of attraction is not sinful per se, but it does make maintaining a platonic perspective difficult. The key is in your commitment to the Friendship/Courtship /Marriage cycle, and in your willingness to forsake some immediate pleasure for future gain. That's where your Christian community can be especially supportive.

The Lost Art of Courtship

So what happens when you discover that friendship is not enough? Some couples who are friends for a while may discover a serious, mutual attraction that they would like to pursue "romantically." Because that sounds so businesslike, I'll put it another way. What if Teresa and Steve begin to feel like they are "falling in love"? In the pattern that I'm suggesting, they would not begin to "date," at least not in the traditional sense of the word. In fact, we would do well to dispense with the idea of "dating" altogether. Instead, Teresa and Steve would begin to "court." I know that may sound like a hopelessly out-of-date idea, but I mean to propose a new vision of "courtship" that shows how different it is from "dating" in motive, expectations, and practice. They are as dissimilar as whole grain rice is from instant rice. Dating, too, is a counterfeit; it may taste okay at first, but it doesn't have any substance.

Here is the difference in rather stark, hard terms. Dating is misdirected illusion; it is as an end in itself. Dating is about play-acting marriage without enjoying all its benefits or committing to its responsibilities. Courtship focuses on marriage. Romance will be part of the experience, but it is not the intended goal. In dating, jealous possessiveness is expected. In courtship, the couple is trying to discover if some form of *healthy* possessiveness (marriage) is in their future. Courtship is a conscious, mutual, evaluative movement toward a marriage that is based on friendship.

Although we cannot always easily categorize our attractions and our intentions, the difference in perspective will affect our choices. People expect that their *dating* "careers" will include a series of sexual and emotional attachments and subsequent detachments. Those who *court* anticipate that they may commit to courtship only once in a lifetime (though given current relational patterns, this would be rare). In dating, couples ask, "What can we do to have romantic fun?" In courtship, couples say, "Sure, let's have some romantic fun—but let's also find out if we are right for each other."

Have I made courtship out to be a drab, strictly rational examination of a couple's compatibility quotient? *I hope not.* The excitement of contemplating marriage and beginning to sort through the implications of spending a lifetime together is intense and wonderful. Is courtship just a morally sanctioned version of dating? Is it: "As long as we don't date over and over again, it's okay?" No. Courtship may add the seriousness of potential vow-making (and baby-making) but it does not subtract the joys of romantic attraction.

There will be some similarities between dating and courtship. As couples court, the characteristics of dating—exclusiveness, privacy, romance, and physical expressions of intimacy—will become more noticeable. Courtship obviously entails spending significant time together and thinking of each other in more personal terms. Yet, even though the casual nature of dating is replaced in courtship by a more sincere, evaluative orientation, the prohibitions against physical and emotional fornication (so often ignored in dating) still hold. Although the desire for physical contact seems to grow with a will of its own, Christians must avoid "even a hint of sexual immorality" (Eph. 5:3) and, specifically, situations igniting a fire that can only be quenched in sexual intercourse.

While courtship encourages the growth of emotional commitment and accountability, Christians ought to resist their yearning to be "wedded" to the beloved. To give the other the freedom you have no right to restrict, you must suppress your desire to grasp and possess. You might rephrase the sexual question in these terms: "How far can I go *emotionally?*" The safest response would be to go only as far as will allow you to remain free to act as a single person, as spontaneously as God desires—*and* to respect and encourage that impulse in the other person. What harm will come to you if you live out your desires prematurely? The modern litany of relational chaos may become your personal recitation. What harm will come to you if you suppress the urge to live out all your physical and emotional desires? None. We all have to suppress certain desires every day. (For example, I may have to put off my coffee break so I can finish this chapter.) In fact, the waiting may make the fulfillment all the sweeter.

The more I talk to students about their dating experiences and see their pain and guilt, the more motivated I become to recommend a different way to prepare for marriage. Although wooing-toward-wedlock has no built-in guarantee against overstated dreams and clammy hands, the advantages of courtship make it a compelling option. For one thing, the implication that marriage is a distinct possibility increases the chance that the courting pair will welcome feedback from more mature couples or even seek formal advice from a Christian counselor. Courtship is an arrangement into which one does not enter lightly. Because courtship's link to marriage makes it less likely to be an on-again/off-again involvement than "going steady" often is, courtship blesses friendship. Instead of all heterosexual relationships operating "on trial," tormented by the other's exacting checklist, the evaluative experience is restricted to courtship. Relieved of such pressure, precourtship friends can be free to enjoy each other's company, and courting couples can honor, and not be threatened by, the platonic aspect of their relationship.

All in all, courting couples would seem more likely to make informed marriage commitments than couples whose vision is clouded by romantic fairly tales. Filled with the knowledge of the other in a variety of character-revealing circumstances and open to the constructive criticism of loving friends, courting couples tend to base their choices regarding marriage on secure foundations.

Courtship is such a serious stage in a relationship that it is logical to ask, "How will we know when to begin courting?" Since any human relationship is somewhat of a "mystery" in that it has many undefinable elements unique to the individuals involved, the best I can do is respond rather obscurely and hope you get the point. When should you enter courtship? *When you can do nothing else.* When—out of your desire to act wisely instead of upon the whimsy of infatuation—you can suppress your attraction no longer. When—after experiencing the richness of friendship—the potential of marriage seems an appropriate idea to explore. Courtship actually begins when you are ready to acknowledge that, barring unforeseen complications, the two of you will *probably* get married. Sounds simple, huh?

Having remained friends long enough to test their basic compatibility, couples then may choose to test the possibility of marriage. Courtship is romance *for the sake of marriage,* a phase that one enters humbly, acknowledging all that is necessary to forge a strong marriage. Courtship is a nerve-racking, tenuous, discomforting challenge. It is also a wonderfully exciting period of life.

Breaking the Pattern

So, now what? What if the ideas in this chapter ring so true that you are ready to live them out? What if, after years of "dating," you are ready to ask, "How do I stop this emotional fornication?" (Most of you won't say that out loud!) You probably already think of going away to college as a time to begin anew, to develop a different (and improved) reputation, to break out of old habits. It is also a good time to begin a revised approach to relationships. Here are some suggestions that will help you get started on that personal makeover.

First, changing your perspective requires a clear sense of where you are headed and what you want to avoid. In a culture that drenches you with messages to the contrary, you will more faithfully remain steadfast if you keep a destination in sight. If you decide that you want to reject emotional fornication and accept the courtship model, consider what images will keep that vision before you and what propositions will remind you of the way you would like to go. Take specific steps to resist the obsession with sensual romance that exists in our world. For example, laugh at the commercials that claim that romance equals happiness or that chewing this gum or driving that car (etc.) will make you irresistible to just about everyone. Temptations tend to recede under the light of truth, especially when the brightness is applied with humor. Martin Luther once remarked that the proud spirit of Satan cannot endure to be mocked. As we explored in chapter 4, Christians are called to *both* hate evil and cling to the good. Although romance is a gift from God and therefore is not "evil" it has been inflated to proportions that resemble idolatry. If you can recognize the idol, will you knock it off its pedestal?

Second, recognize that in a world with an unheavenly bent, living by faith is not just a matter of bearing down and "doing good" with gritted teeth. Trusting God about relationships is as difficult as trusting him about other matters. You can be certain that you will sometimes experience failure, that you will require his mercy and patience often. Most of us carry a substantial amount of guilt about past relationships. With the weight of this burden on our shoulders, many of us have become deformed, even crippled. We need healing and transformation, not merely the removal of the load. And, indeed, this is what God promises. If you renew your faith in Jesus as the Healer and Helper that you need, his grace will abound.

Third, I have become convinced that the Friendship/Courtship plan may not be achievable outside the context of Christian fellowship. As Os Guinness has said, pursuing a way of life contrary to prevailing social norms requires a community that also operates contrary to those norms. Without much imagination, you can probably see the difficulties of trying to replace dating with the friendship approach in a social environment that accepts dating as the appropriate pattern for heterosexual relationships. How could this be accomplished without a support system? My students have told me that, after discussing this point of view with others, they made an overt commitment to form a group for men and women who wanted to spend time together without the pressure of pairing up. Romances sometimes developed, but the confirmed values and dedication to friendship within the group make it much easier for individuals to avoid "emotional fornication."

Finally, remember that the joy of significant, loving relationships is always within your reach. Is American-style dating a necessary prerequisite for deep sharing and emotional intimacy? No. Although you will need to be on guard against subjects and situations that are physically and emotionally seductive, the heavenly conversation of kindred souls, where eternal truths are discussed and treasured, is even more attainable. The courtship perspective sets you free to pursue that joy.

The concept of emotional fornication is not merely a curious play on words. The simple reminder comes: we reap what we sow. During an age when countless relational disasters cause many to refer to themselves as "damaged goods," we would do well to heed the apostle Paul's admonition toward peace and encouragement.

What's in Your Heart?

1. What correlation can you see between marital problems and the four characteristics of dating described in this chapter?

2. Do you believe that dating is emotional fornication? Is it sinful? Defend your case.
3. If you were to adopt the Friendship/Courtship/ Marriage plan, how would your current relationships be affected?

Part Four
The Intellectual (!) Christian

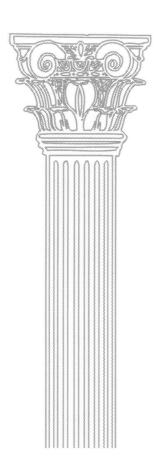

What? I'm Also Expected to Think?

> Man is only a reed, the weakest in nature, but he is a thinking reed. . . . [All] our dignity consists in thought. . . . Let us then strive to think well.
>
> Blaise Pascal

Come to think of it, do I really need to put in a good word about thinking, especially in a book that will probably be read by only the most serious and highly motivated college students? What could be more natural, more important, more praiseworthy than thinking? What elevates us above the beasts? (Opposable thumbs would do us little good if the human brain were the size of a pea.) What could be more obvious than to realize that being made in God's image grants us "higher intelligence": the ability to reason, solve abstract problems, and discover the meaning of our existence?

155

Yet, in modern America, "thinking" is not in good repute. Some are prone to agree with the late artist Andy Warhol when he said, "If I had my way I'd paint Campbell soup cans every day. It's just so easy and you don't have to think. It's just too hard to think." Of course, Warhol was right. Thinking can be real work. This in itself may be a deterrent. In a culture that has glorified leisure, created a huge market for any book with the words "Made Easy" in its title, and discovered that nothing is as irritating as not being able to find the TV's remote control, work is not necessarily appealing. Even if we acknowledge the worth of our ability to think, many of us are skeptical of anyone who seems to overstate its importance. We may be grateful that we can think well enough to read, shop, or converse or hold a job, yet believe that something is abnormal about people who are "intellectual." Is this consistent?

Thinking about Thinking in a Non-thinking Culture

Are Americans wary of the intellect? Are we prejudiced against those who excel with the mind? One such intellectual person, Vaclav Havel, a playwright, was elected to the presidency of post-Communist Czechoslovakia. Could that happen here? One way to answer this question is to explore your own recent experience. Who had more statue in your high school: the athletes and cheerleaders or the scholars? Which of these phrases sounds more familiar: "What a nerd. He's always got his nose in a book" or "What a jerk. He's always admiring what he sees in the mirror." More personally, what would you rather be known for: your intelligence or your physical attractiveness?

No, I don't *think* that thinking is prized by most people in our society. Many have written about the decrepit state of the life of the mind. Among others, Allan Bloom in *The Closing of the American Mind* and E. D. Hirsch in *Cultural Literacy* have spoken worriedly about our educational defi-

ciencies. Bloom says: "People sup together, play together, travel together, but they do not think together. Hardly any homes have any intellectual life whatsoever, let alone one that informs the vital interests of life." Would you say that your family has an "intellectual life"? Does the very question have an odd ring to it?

A few years ago, I visited the marvelous American History Museum in Washington, D.C., in which the artifacts of our nation are arranged chronologically. As I walked through the rooms, I was struck by an abrupt shift in emphasis in the early twentieth century. The primary artifacts from the pre-1920 era are examples of fine craftsmanship (Shaker furniture or Williamsburg pewter) or influential documents (Paine's *Common Sense* or Stowe's *Uncle Tom's Cabin*). For the modern era, entertainment-related items dominate the display cases: the bat of Babe Ruth, the ruby slippers of Oz, the glove of Michael Jackson. Without denigrating all of popular culture, the question deserves attention: Does this shift tell a story of a dwindling interest in the life of the mind?

Too many Americans act as if the creative thinkers of the past never existed or, at best, have little relevance in today's world. Much of this knowledge used to be considered normative. As a professor, I must deal with the effects of this anti-intellectualism every day. When I consider which examples will resonate with most of my students, I find that I cannot refer to Mark Twain or the Bible or Shakespeare or C. S. Lewis or Mozart or St. Augustine or Martin Luther (unless, of course, these folks have been portrayed in a recent movie). However, I can be confident of getting a resonant reaction if I mention Bart Simpson or Bill Cosby or Janet Jackson or Stephen King. For this generation, "Calvin" is not the great Protestant Reformer of the sixteenth century but a stegosaurus-haired comic-strip character with a stuffed tiger for a friend. "Michelangelo" is not a Renaissance painter and sculptor but a mutated reptile who eats pizza. What's more, few students seem to be concerned about their ignorance of the past. They want even learning to take the form of flashy and ever-pleasant show biz. It's not that entertainment is evil. It's just that we seem to neglect just about everything else. For instance, when was the last Friday night you voluntarily spent an evening in what might be called mental exercise?

Most modern Americans are suspicious of the thinker and believe that anyone who worries about every jot and tittle of every question is not being sufficiently "practical." In the fast-paced and interpersonally demanding nineties, we often act as if thinking is a waste of time, a frivolous luxury that runs against the grain of true egalitarian democracy. An intellectual is seen as presumptuous, an egghead, a snooty highbrow.

It is no different in the church. Pastors are often criticized for "talking over our heads," or for what amounts to the same thing: "being dull." We are more likely to hear about "Be Happy" attitudes or the Ten Suggestions than any thoroughgoing theology. Yet the writer of Hebrews chastised early Christian converts for keeping their theology so simplistic that it was suitable for only spiritual infants. "Quit sucking that bottle!" is the message of Hebrews 5:13–14. Similarly, J. I. Packer, author of *Knowing God,* calls the church's anti-intellectualism "jacuzzi religion." He writes: "The jacuzzi experience is sensuous, relaxing, floppy, laid-back: not in any way demanding, whether intellectually or otherwise, but very, very nice, even to the point of being great fun. . . . Many want religion to be like that, and labour to make it so."

Evidence of this reluctance to think is not difficult to find in the Christian community. What kind of publications dominate the best-seller lists of religious books? Mainly self-help manuals and biographies of Christian celebrities. What kind of books are your personal favorites? If you could take only five books with you to a deserted island, what would you take besides the Bible? Can you name five books that are important to you? As you consider your list, do you expect these books to be cherished for years to come?

What about the Bible itself? Do you groan when the pastor says that he will be preaching out of the Book of Romans for two months? Church leaders of the past were *theologians* of depth as well as models of spiritual vitality. Because evangelicals tend to emphasize the emotional rather than the intellectual aspects of Christianity, strenuous Bible study may be neglected in modern church life. That may be one reason why, when compared to today's "pop"theology, Jonathan Edwards' sermons, John Milton's poetry, and Charles Wesley's hymns seem overbearingly complex. When addressing Wheaton College graduates, Charles Malik, former ambassador to the United Nations from Lebanon, said:

> I must be frank with you: the greatest danger confronting American evangelical Christianity is the danger of anti-intellectualism. The mind in its greatest and deepest reaches is not cared for enough. People who are in a hurry to get out of the university and start earning money or serving the church or preaching the gospel have no idea of the infinite value of spending years of leisure conversing with the greatest minds and souls of the past, ripening and sharpening and enlarging their powers of thinking.

Lest those of you who suspect you are ignoring your "powers of thinking" begin to feel too guilty, I hasten to add that this state of things is not entirely your fault. You should not be blamed for living in an age so entertainment-oriented that it thinks Doonesbury is philosophy that rivals Plato or Kant. Nor should you be held responsible for the quality of the education you have received. You may hope that college will make up for part of this deficit. It may, but a love for learning, a heart for truth, will not develop automatically (or even be encouraged) once you enroll in college courses.

Many in the church have lost the passion to understand God's world. Even for those who care or are beginning to care, it is a quality that needs significant nurturing. There are at least two stages in the recovery of respect for the mind. First, there must be a sense of need to motivate us. Second, there must be a constructive response to that need.

Thinking for Christians
Who Aren't Sure about Thinking

Although college is not exactly a foolproof Get Smart Quick scheme, the total experience can be a Muscle Beach for the Mind. One of my greatest joys as a professor is to provide a catalyst and then watch a sleeping or lazy mind awaken. If students flex their mental muscles long enough and with enough strain (no pain, no gain), growth will be noticeable. Unfortunately, many students are not convinced that the strain is worth it. Unless they contemplate grad school, they are satisfied with barely passing grades, believing they can still be a success at home, church, and business without having an intellectual orientation. Such has not always been the case. Historian Jaroslav Pelikan wrote, "Once upon a time—and a very good time it was—being an intellectual meant being a Christian."

What reasons are there for "average" college students to be enthusiastic about making progress in thinking? There are scores of Scripture verses and pages of other books that have been devoted to supplying ample rationale for a healthy pursuit of the truth.(Some of which is listed in Recommended Reading, p. 229.) Their collective wisdom can be summarized under two headings that will warm you up for the collegiate examination process.

True or False?—"All Christians Are Called On to Develop the Mind"

Please note that this is not a multiple choice question. "Many," "some," or "a few" are not among the options. As much as some might declare that one's Christian life is wholly "spiritual", something to do only with prayer and

Bible study, Jesus says that faith is at least partly about using our heads. And using them even about many ordinary issues. For example, Jesus says that those who worry about clothes lack faith because they are not thinking clearly (Matt. 6:28–30): "If that is how God clothes the grass of the field, which is here today and tomorrow is thrown into the fire, will he not much more clothe you, O you of little faith?" He describes here a direct relationship between faith and reason. "Figure it out," Jesus is saying. "Your ability to reason should teach you that if the Father cares for the less significant, he would also care for the more significant." Of course, this verse is only a small part of the larger command to love God with our minds. There are at least four reasons to love God in this way.

First, *we must love God with our minds because God wants our entire beings to be devoted to him.* To divide intellect from soul is to say that there is a part of us that is outside of God's influence or restorative powers. Those who separate mind and spirit are not only trying to achieve an impossibility (as if we could worship or learn from the Scriptures without our minds), but they are denying the sovereignty of God, disobeying Christ's call to follow him in all respects, and artificially limiting the role of faith. To say that God wants every part of us to be subordinated to him is also to say that all aspects of our true selves are being sanctified, transformed into his likeness. Paul puts the mind at the center of that process: "Be transformed by the renewing of your mind. Then you will be able to test and approve what God's will is—his good, pleasing and perfect will" (Rom. 12:2b). If we *think* well about God and others we will be more likely to live well. If we think clearly about God's kingdom, we are more likely to understand what is going on and what to do. We cannot neglect the mind and expect to become better disciples. What most embarrasses us about Christian leaders? Foolishness. Besides fraud and sexual improprieties, we have to put up with such unresponsible analyses as the one saying that God is holding off Armageddon so that the church can make a killing in the stock market.

Second, *we are to love God with our minds because we are to be good stewards of all that we have been given.* This relates to the "fulfilling our potential" reason for going to college (see chapter 1). It is no small matter that our ability to draw conclusions, make relationships, solve problems, and exercise creativity is part of what it means to be made in God's image. To be transformed into his likeness is to become more true to his image in us, including our thinking skills and the conclusions resulting from those abilities. Paul writes that believers "have put on the new self, which is being renewed in knowledge in the image of its Creator" (Col. 3:10). For a human to disparage thinking would be like a dolphin to deny the worth of swimming.

Third, *as our minds learn better how to love God, we are less likely to follow happily along with every slip and slide of our culture.* The introduction to the Romans 12:2 passage mentioned earlier reads: "Do not conform any longer to the pattern of this world." Jesus prayed that his disciples would be *in* but not *of* this world (John 17:13–19). From the beginning of the Old Testament to the end of the New, the Word of God speaks continually of God's people being set apart and therefore not succumbing to the ungodly ways that surround them. How can we resist the subtle but powerful lies of our culture if we cannot recognize them? Anyone could spot a red-suited Satanist. But what about a sweat-suited hedonist? Or a silk-suited materialist? Subtle cultural deceptions about the mind can exist anywhere. Even in college you will encounter Christians whose attitude is: "Don't give me this intellectual stuff. All I need is Jesus!" Will these anti-intellectual believers be able to discern what is happening to them as they sit uncritically in front of the TV for four hours every night? The mind must be fully operative if we are to see and resist the world's ploys and enticements.

Fourth, and perhaps least appreciated of all, *we are to love God with our minds out of gratitude that we are able to do so*. The joy and privilege of deep thought is sometimes lost on a culture too impatient to contemplate. Paul gives us delightful latitude: ". . . whatever is true, whatever is noble, whatever is right, whatever is pure, whatever is lovely, whatever is admirable—if anything is excellent or praiseworthy—think about such things" (Phil. 4:8). He was partly telling the Philippians not to think about ungodly things, but he was also affirming that all truth is God's truth. There is a stimulating, enjoyable, edifying universe of God's making out there, waiting for our mental gifts to engage with it. God has not made us to be computers who can only obey fixed programs. The call to "think" is not a punishment or even a duty; it is a gift too remarkable to be squandered. As I watch my daughters learn everything from the alphabet to riding a bicycle, I am enthralled, amazed, and proud. The human mind is so incredible and we can have so much fun using it that surely our heavenly Father is just as excited when *we* learn. If the angels rejoice over the salvation of a lost soul, maybe they sing a few tunes when an anxious disciple stares hard at a flower and suddenly realizes, "I guess God will take care of me, too."

Essay Question: "Are Some Christians Particularly Called to Be Thinkers?"

Contrary to the approach of popular Christianity, I believe we should answer this essay question in the affirmative. Although all are called to think, some do have a special calling to pursue wisdom, just as all are called to evangelize, but some have a special gift for evangelism. As the response to this essay question is developed, issues of what and why and who will be addressed.

What would it mean to be "particularly called" to be thinkers? Jaroslav Pelikan says that the three marks of the Christian thinker are "a passion for being because the Father is the Creator and Source of all being; a reverence for language because Jesus Christ is the Word and Mind of the Father; an enthusiasm for history because the Holy Spirit works through history to produce variety and to unite all men to himself." Some in the church are noticeably gifted with these characteristics.

Another characteristic of the "intellectual Christian" is suggested in the Old Testament. In one list of the various tribes of Israel, the text cites "the men of Issachar, who understood the times and knew what Israel should do . . ." (1 Chron. 12:32). Although God's people are no longer assigned roles by tribes, might there be a precedent here for acknowledging a particular calling to the life of the mind? To whom will we turn for insight about our times if there are no gifted and dedicated Christian thinkers?

Why would some be "particularly called"? Most New Testament descriptions of the body of Christ express the idea that we all have different functions within the community of believers. Though one function has no more status than another, neither should any role be ignored. Everyone has at least one special job to do.

One need within the church is to understand the complexities of life on all levels. We are not equally gifted to construct biblical theology or answer an unbeliever's challenging rebuke. Those who struggle to understand perplexing matters need stronger brothers and sisters to assist them. If Christians neglect important intellectual questions, the answers are often left to those who have contrary values; so the church needs help discerning where it is accommodating unbiblically to the surrounding culture. The church needs its thinkers, even though they are sometimes a nuisance. In the recent Persian Gulf War, most Americans thought that once the conflict began, no one should be critical of the country's efforts. Yet some brave thinkers raised questions about the aftermath of such a contest. The church is in danger whenever it takes a purposefully uncritical stance toward national or worldwide events. As the refugee situation unfolded in the Middle East, many Americans realized that the American strategy was not without flaws. In his book *The Christian Mind,* Harry Blamires writes:

> The thinker challenges current prejudices. He disturbs the complacent. He obstructs the busy pragmatists. He questions the very foundations of all those around him, and in so doing throws doubt upon aims, motives and purposes which those who are running affairs have neither time nor patience to investigate.

Who might be among those "particularly called"? You probably could guess by now: *you* (well, maybe). Although you may be going to college merely to avoid other less comfortable options, you may also be recognizing a certain kind of giftedness. You don't have to be an Einstein to be considered a thinker. (After all, even Einstein wasn't an Einstein about everything.) The more important characteristic for you might be a certain resonance with Pelikan's passion for being, reverence for language, or enthusiasm for history. Other telltale signs include the enjoyment of education, a sense of reward from intellectual tasks well accomplished, and an appreciation for the subtleties of ideas that you know others do not share. Do you delight in a rousing discussion? When you think of a solution to a problem or an answer to a tough question, are you anxious to share your response or put it to some use? You may be "particularly called."

Whether or not you feel called to be a thinker, others with less education will assume that you should perform this function within the body of believers. Because you will be seen as part of the "thinking arm" (thinking cap?) of the church, perhaps the best way for you to serve the Lord is through what C. S. Lewis called "the learned life." Lewis was once asked during World War II how those in school could justify their studies when their countrymen were being killed on the battlefield. In *The Weight of Glory,* he answered thus:

> To be ignorant and simple now—not to be able to meet the enemies on their own ground—would be to throw down our weapons, and to betray our uneducated brethren who have, under God, no defense but us against the intellectual attacks of the heathen. Good philosophy must exist, if for no other reason, because bad philosophy needs to be answered. . . . The learned life then is, for some, a duty. At the moment it looks as if it were your duty.

Though you may not be convinced of your intellectual giftedness at present, college is a wonderful place to explore that possibility. If for no other reason than to test your calling, I would encourage you to devote yourself for the time being to the life of the mind.

Thinking for Christians Who Are Ready to Think

Now that you've taken that two-part "exam," do you see where you fit in? Are you ready to consider the role of the "thinking Christian"? Though you may not be prepared to write twelve volumes of systematic theology and cultural analysis, you may be more intellectual than you realize.

Once motivated, Christians need some idea of what it means to be a thinker. It doesn't require you to frame your grade reports or wow your friends with your vocabulary or undefeated record in Trivial Pursuit. A few pages back, I suggested that anti-intellectuals in the church tend to divide mind from soul; that is, they believe that true spirituality has little or nothing to do with the intellect. The converse is also a current trend: Some thinkers act as if the mind should not be influenced by the soul. In your courses, you have probably met students who compete well for grades but whose faith seems irrelevant to their studies. Those who "love God with the mind" are not merely good students by the world's standards. Christian thinkers do not strive strictly to achieve academically (though that goal is worthy), but to have their ideas and discussions informed by the mind of Christ. This theological orientation suggests that Christian reasoning is not only about mental skills. To think as a Christian means to think as Christ would have us think and to reach conclusions that Christ would have us reach. As Harry Blamires contends, there are two prerequisites to the achievement of a Christian mind: A Christian "frame of reference" and a Christian "field of discussion."

Your *frame of reference* is the set of presuppositions that informs your thinking. When you decide to vote for candidate A, buy a specific car, or write from a certain perspective in a term paper, what ideas direct your choice? Do Christ's concerns dominate—or do Walt Disney's or MTV's or the professor's? Does biblical theology influence your conclusions or does something else, such as pragmatism or complacency? When it comes to politics, if you think of yourself as a Democrat or Republican *first*, your politics will be Democrat or Republican, not Christian. If your approach to consumer goods is as an acquiring American (who is entitled to anything you can afford) and not as a Christian *first*, your purchases will reflect those values. Blamires's contention is that modern Christians are so secularized that they have no idea they are following cultural standards instead of Christ.

What would Christ-focused thinking look like? Many authors suggest systems for organizing a Christian frame of reference, but Blamires names six "marks of the Christian mind"—a supernatural orientation, an awareness of evil, an objective conception of truth, an acceptance of authority, a concern for the person, and a sacramental cast. These marks, he says, represent a frame of reference that is thoroughly biblical and thoroughly applicable. For example, from a supernatural orientation, a Christian thinker realizes that earthly success is not the most important measure of a person. He or she recognizes the superficiality of celebrity status or a dream house when viewed through the lens of eternity.

Although there isn't space here to do more than invite you to pursue the many writings on this subject, I will caution you not to assume that your frame of reference is in good condition. You will probably discover this soon enough in your courses, especially if you are challenged about what you (not your parents or pastor or friends) believe. Too often, Christians seem arrogant or defensive about what they know, instead of humble about what they don't know. For example, how have you responded to the suggestion that your frame of reference may need development? Are you intrigued—or threatened? "Intrigued" is a good sign because it demonstrates a thirst to know, but this thirst does not automatically produce rain clouds of insightful thoughts. A Christian frame of reference will not descend upon you from the sky any more than will the answers to this week's World Civilization quiz. For both, you must first be properly motivated and then apply yourself to the task. If you have any sense that your frame of reference is thin, you would do well to eat heartily from the table of Scripture. Paul commended this study to Timothy: "All Scripture is God-breathed and is useful for teaching, rebuking, correcting and training in righteousness, so that the man of God may be thoroughly equipped for every good work" (2 Tim. 3:16–17).

A *field of discussion,* according to Blamires, is a vibrant, ongoing conversation with like-minded believers. It is a place where we can go to discuss any issues, from politics to business, through the lens of our Christian frame of reference. To think truly as Christians, we need not only solid biblical ideas to inform our decision, but friends with whom we can talk about the way we are applying our frame of reference. For example, do you have friends with whom you can discuss an advertising campaign that you believe degrades women? Are you confident that these friends will speak out of a Christian frame of reference?

Over the years, I have often promoted discussions of lecture material outside the classroom. One class dubbed these sessions "Hemingway over Hamburgers." Although many a lighthearted lunch hour has been spent mainly joking about the latest dorm adventure, some meals—and lives— have been enriched because students felt free to talk about more serious matters as well.

Some of the above may sound rather strongly stated at times, but what I'm telling you is something you already know: Yes, you *are* expected to think. And *how* you think will determine the kind of person you become in the future. I hope that your campus experiences will include both structured and seemingly "accidental" forums—dialogues with kindred spirits with whom you share a Christ-centered approach to wisdom. "Intellectual" and "Christian" are not contradictory terms.

What's in Your Heart?

1. Where would you place yourself and your family on a scale of "very intellectual" to "anti-intellectual"? Do you wish these placements would change?
2. What does it mean to "love God with your mind"? When have you been certain that you did this?
3. What evidence have you experienced that would suggest that the life of the mind might be something to which you are "particularly called"?

12 Enemies of the Thinking Christian

A thinking man should always attack the strongest thing in his own time because the strongest thing is always too strong.

G. K. Chesterton

The first time I went to do research in graduate school, I was encouraged to see familiar words in stone above the entrance to the University of Oregon library: "The truth shall make you free." I soon discovered, however, that the "truth" presented in the courses was as elusive as it is in political campaigns. The slogan should have read: "You shall create your own truth, and the truth shall enable you to do as you please, providing that you don't hurt anyone else." Maybe they didn't want to use that much stone.

The limited vision of truth that one finds in many educational institutions can

171

also be found within certain holier-than-thou halls of the church. Many fellowships seem to say that as long as you have "accepted Jesus as your Savior," all is well. When understood in its fullest sense, this is true. Unfortunately, what such groups mean is that as long as you participate in the right number of church-related activities, what you do the rest of the time doesn't matter.

I once asked a stockbroker, who was also a deacon at his church, how he dealt with the troubling ethical dilemma of recommending investments in companies that he knew had corrupt practices. His answer was: "My pastor told me that *my* job was to make money for my clients—God would deal with any wrongdoing." Or take the report in *Leadership* magazine that during a convention for youth pastors, the hotel broke its record for X-rated movie rentals. Christians who are so casually amoral or immoral are showing how little their principles affect their day-to-day choices.

Does our faith not require that we follow Christ instead of our culture? As Chesterton's remark implies, the thinker should identify what is overstated in the culture and resist it. How can we be *in* the world, yet not *of* it, unless we study that world and compare its values to God's? Is not this kind of analysis part of what it means to love God with our minds?

The work of Christian thinkers is never easy and rarely appreciated. A variety of "enemies" make their task difficult, lonely, and at times even spiritually dangerous. Perhaps the greatest hazard to the American Christian lies in the inclination to conform to culture, even in areas where this amounts to a denial or rejection of biblical truths. We might call this type of conformity "accommodation," for it is a merging of godly and ungodly principles.

The Church as Chameleon

Most of us have admired the remarkably adaptable qualities of that weird-eyed lizard, the chameleon. Wouldn't it be great to be able to blend in so perfectly wherever we go? Although the possibilities are fascinating, one tragedy of our times is that the *church* has too successfully become a chameleon. It tends to take on the prevailing culture's coloration, even when doing so results in a shade unlike Christ's hue.

One cause of this reptilian imitation is a hazy sense of the church's role in the world. Malcolm Muggeridge writes, "Of all the distortions of Scripture—and heaven knows there have been plenty in our time—the most disastrous is surely to suggest that when our Lord insisted that his kingdom was not of this world, he meant that it was." Yet, if we look back on previous eras in church history, we should be embarrassed by how agreeably the church has imitated its environment. Why did the Christian establishment endorse so many wars and so much violence, including the brutality of the Crusades, the persecution of the Jews, and the enslavement of whole nations? Where was the Christian in Nazi Germany? The more important questions are: "How is the church accommodating *now*? Are most of us chameleons, or willing to tolerate them?"

A few quick examples. It is not surprising that in an era devoted to financial gain, there are so many preachers who espouse a Gospel of Prosperity, as if Jesus' strongest desire is to make life materially easy for believers and to reward the faithful with BMWs and hefty bank accounts. Isn't he more concerned about mercy, justice, faith, and spiritual contentment than financial acquisition? Or take our distorted view of fellowship. If the church cannot be distinguished from the local country club, hasn't there been a serious misunderstanding of the Lord's version of discipleship? More personally, where do you get your sense of worth? If you merely adopt the common value that "image is everything," have you not accommodated to culture instead of having been transformed by the renewal of your mind? Does your status before God count less than your popularity or physical attractiveness? Do you care enough about the *inner* person to risk being rejected or ridiculed for your belief in Christ?

Whom do you admire? Do you accept our culture's version of success: that material wealth, fame, or business status is the height of achievement? Society often implies that even immoral people may be admirable. Many popular movies and television shows present the bad guys as the good guys, encouraging us to root for evil to triumph. Likewise, we may have seen so much promiscuity on the screen that we are embarrassed by chastity. These kinds of comparisons between personal values and cultural values provide some measure of accommodation to "the world."

The desire to blend, to be chameleons, is in all of us. If we don't want to be noticed and risk being rejected, we will probably be tempted to merge imperceptibly into our surroundings. It is much harder to live out your Christian convictions by choosing only the colors in keeping with God's kingdom. If you find that you are not conscious of any accommodation, my guess is that you have already changed your skin so many times that you are now color blind.

The Enemies Within

Pridefulness

"Knowledge puffs up, but love builds up. The man who thinks he knows something does not yet know as he ought to know. But the man who loves God is known by God" (1 Cor. 8:1–3). Though we are called to reason as disciples of Christ, we are quite capable of doing it poorly. In the above passage and others (see Col. 3:18, for example), Paul describes what can happen to those who take excessive pride in their thinking ability. We love to flaunt whatever seems to make us better than anyone else. An intellectual champion is no less likely to make Clint Eastwood's boast, "Go ahead. Make my day."

Besides accommodation, the enemies of the Christian thinker are many. Some come from within the thinker, arising from some abuse of the virtue of loving God with the mind. Other foes come from outside the thinker, enemies that challenge even those Christians who pursue bold, heavenly colors.

Certainly, one of the dangers of becoming competent in anything is the temptation to be vain and pretentious. Knowledge *can* puff up. Haven't you ever thrust your hand in the air in the classroom to show off your enviable insight? The more we know, the more we may think that this somehow makes us more valuable to God, superior to lesser creatures. In Dorothy L. Sayers's play *The Zeal of Thy House,* the architect William proclaims:

> We are the master of craftsmen, God and I—
> We understand one another. None, as I can,
> Can creep under the ribs of God, and feel
> His heart beat through those Six Days of Creation.

So what can you do about this cunning enemy from within? First, realize that fear of pride is no reason to avoid the pursuit of knowledge. Anything can promote pride— even ignorance! Second, be particularly sensitive to your manifestations of self-importance. The smartest people are not above a triumphant grin, but they may cleverly refrain from advertising their cleverness. Yet, conceit over knowledge is a sure sign of a poor attitude toward learning. If you have approached your studies honestly, you will conclude that the more you know, the humbler you ought to become. Education should force us to acknowledge how little we know, to see God's greatness and our comparative insignificance, and to realize how few of our ideas are fully original. Pascal said, "Reason's last step is the recognition that there are an infinite number of things which are beyond it. It is merely feeble if it does not go as far as to realize that."

Intellectual pride impedes our spiritual progress and therefore the proper use of the mind. Haughtiness is diametrically opposed to faith, because there is little room (or need) for God as we begin to feel full of ourselves for what we know. Then we worship the creation, especially our knowledge of it, instead of the Creator. Ever notice how some students who were proud of being at the top of their class in seventh grade were not up there as high school seniors? Part of the reason is that arrogance disrupts the thinking process. Mental activity is a dynamic that either continues to mature or atrophies. Some know-it-alls believe there is nothing more to know, so they stop trying. Their heart for truth is no longer operating. Others are so inflated by their own grade point average that they lose sight of the true value of learning.

Cynicism

One type of pride that deserves its own designation as an "enemy from within" is *cynicism*. One of the most unpleasant inhabitants of the fields of academia is the Arrogant Prig. This boorish beast does not so much glory in his or her own feats as look down on the accomplishments of everyone else. Favorite comments of the cynic include: "How childish!" "So what!" and "You really believe that?"

Though honest skepticism is healthy and often appropriate, especially when applied to advertising and political discourse, cynicism is a kind of intellectual illness, a perversion of the gift of intelligence. Those cursed with this contagious disease spread its toxins broadly and deeply, destroying hope and confidence along the way. Better to be a sweet-spirited simpleton than a bloated prig! These are not the only two options, thankfully, but perhaps they are hinted at in Jesus' not-to-be-taken-literally but still blood-curdling advice: "If your right eye causes you to sin, gouge it out and throw it away" (Matt. 5:29a). What if our *brain* causes us to sin?

Cynicism is a destroyer because it discourages all innovative thought except in the unusually stouthearted. What can crush the joy of insight faster than a sneer? Lamentably, when we make some progress as a Christian thinker, we are tempted to wiggle an upper lip of disdain at beginners: "You don't know the 63rd of Martin Luther's 95 theses? Tsk, tsk." "Oh, I see that you've come to your own interpretation of Matthew 6. I once believed that, too." How dare we? What right have we to dash others' dreams? Who are we to dismiss ideas and demoralize their advocates because, in our falsely inflated opinion, they are unworthy of consideration?

Brenda Ueland, whose 1938 book has encouraged generations of writers, states, ". . . we start in our lives as little children, full of light and the clearest vision. . . . Then we go to school and then comes on the great army of . . . sneerers . . . and cantankerous friends, and finally that Great Murderer of the Imagination—a world of unceasing, unkind, dinky, prissy, criticalness." One might well ask: Where in this snooty priggishness is the *heart* for truth? A knife may be needed to cut away at falsehood, but a knife for truth is not enough.

There is so much joy to be found in every revelation of God's glorious world that we should caress every true, soulful sentiment. (Why not wonder what *could* be learned from a "naive" interpretation of Matthew 6?) Sometimes the formal educational process tends to diminish our childlike appreciation of the Creator's work. If you have become insensitive to nuance and innocence, my suggestion is to take a walk with a toddler once a week. It's hard to be cynical beside such unfettered enthusiasm for life.

Fear

The last inner enemy in this list, like the demon called Legion (Mark 5:9), shows itself in many ways and by many names, including apathy, indifference, *ennui,* and sloth. In one way or another, all of these attitudes are related to our fearfulness and uncertainties. Fear of failure. Fear of success. Fear of criticism. Fear of taking responsibility for statements made or actions proposed. What if I say the wrong thing? What if someone challenges me? What if I draw attention to myself? What if, by caring, I'm made uncomfortable? What if I'm not liked? The demon called fear restrains the thinker by repressing his or her spontaneity and integrity.

Part of this fear rests in a self-pity that says, "Oh, woe is me, for I am a man of unwitty lips." Or wonders, "Who cursed me with such a kidney bean for a brain?" Fear tends to create a self-fulfilling prophecy. If you don't take risks because of your fear, your thinking does not get refined. So when you do speak, your rough-edged insight confirms that you never should have spoken in the first place. The difficulties of making decisions in the modern world can sometimes produce in us a lingering quality of reluctance to make commitments, to dream, to take chances.

Just as with pride and cynicism, fear destroys the thinking process. Without the hope of getting better, we find motivation difficult to come by. I have had several students tell me (in their senior year of college, no less) that most of their education had been a waste, not so much because their schools were poor, but because they had avoided what true learning might require of them. Some of them had managed to play the "game" of education well, while others merely hobbled from class to class, desperately searching for the easiest route to a passing grade. But all of these students had in common an evasion of new ideas that would force them to leave the security of their apathy. They also shunned any task that obligated them to move from "education as a series of hurdles" to "education as a process for developing a heart for truth."

The way out of this stagnation necessarily involves suffering. The humility strong enough to risk the rejection of one's own perspectives is the only attitude that will get those ideas grounded in wisdom rather than empty speculation or prejudice. If we care about the truth and have a passion for it, we will accept some pain and disappointment. The good news is that a heart for truth can grow quickly if it is spiritually motivated. The more we take risks to refine our thinking, the better it becomes and the freer we feel to take chances, and so on. Fear is cast away by God's perfect love, a love that moves us to learn whatever he would have us learn.

The Enemies around Us

Some enemies of the thinking Christian come from outside. Even if we manage to avoid the inner hazards of pride, cynicism, and fear, we will most likely encounter any number of adversaries who are not pleased with thinking grounded in Christianity. Sound biblical truth and the faith that results from knowing that truth *will* meet with resistance.

Sometimes these enemies around us take the form of alternative claims to truth. In a world that is often described as "post-Christian," you do not have to look hard to find intellectual antagonists who accept neither God nor the Scriptures. As difficult as it may be to confront such straightforward enemies as Marxism, scientism, or pantheism, at least such views present obvious points of conflict. You may have to work hard to understand and contend with these ideas, but the differences are no mystery. Many of you will write papers that take issue with these ideologies. I can see the titles now: "From G. B. Shaw to B. F. Skinner: 100 years of Harsh Words for Christians," or "Why the New-Age Movement Fails to Answer Age-Old Problems."

Since you will probably be challenged to address these outspoken foes in the natural course of your studies, I would like to highlight a few external "enemies" that are subtler and more covert in their strategy. Like spies, these enemies approach us as friends, earning our trust and then—when they have our confidence—they betray us. There are at least three types of subversives that will attempt to infiltrate your thinking and destroy your faith.

Spies that Make You See Green: Materialism

UCLA researchers have been studying the values of college freshmen for over twenty years. In a recent survey, nearly 68 percent of the subjects said that a "very important" reason for attending college was "to be able to make more money." The conclusion was "Being well off financially has thus risen from ninth place in 1970 to second place among personal values expressed by freshmen." Although it is no crime to take stock of the future in an increasingly competitive economy, I wonder what prompts this trend more: economic realities or scheming dreams for wealth and leisure. One spy in our midst is the materialist, a grand saboteur who would have us view the world through the green-colored lens of money.

The thought of greed skulking behind the scenes raises a question posed in an earlier chapter: "Why are you going to college?" I received a poster in the mail from General Motors that answers this question succinctly. Above a sleek, sexy Camaro runs a descriptive slogan: "The Rewards of a Higher Education." So that's it! All those years I naively thought I was supposed to be learning something, I could have put my educational gears in neutral and merely coasted along so I could get a car. I wonder whether Chevrolet would have accepted my diploma in exchange for a Z-28!

Materialism, the idea that life's ultimate meaning can be found only through the senses, is so rampant in our culture that we are likely to be blind to its dangerous side effects. In this respect, the campaign of espionage on behalf of materialism has been successful. We may click our tongues in disapproval over the opulence of Donald Trump, but fail to recognize our own lust for his life-style. So long as we are not extremely garish consumers, we think we are not materialistic. Yet we express our secret covetousness in a variety of ways. How much time do you spend ogling clothes or cars that you hope may one day be yours? How many of your evaluations of others are related to their material "good taste"? How impressed are you with possessions? Do you swagger a bit when you know others look with longing on your fancy shirt or new blouse, or the expensive college you attend?

One measure of a materialist culture is the way it refers to notions of *poverty*. In spite of having more possessions than most of the world has ever seen, we may tell our friends that we have "nothing to wear" or that having a five-year-old car means we're "in the poorhouse" or "poverty stricken." Compared to Prince Charles and Scrooge McDuck, yes; but we have things significantly out of perspective if we think we are impoverished unless we have a Mercedes and live in a Tudor mansion—or even if we believe those things will make us content.

Materialism sneaks into our thinking by overstating the values of physical pleasure and making us too expediency minded. It would have us believe that happiness lies in the advertising media's definition of "the good life." This idea is captured in a familiar slogan: "You only go around once in life, so grab for all the gusto you can get." Although pleasure *is* a gift from God, seeking it can become so perverted that we look with disdain upon any activity remotely uncomfortable. As money-making rises on our list of priorities, other more important matters are neglected, including relationships. People may lie to get a promotion, ignore friends and family in pursuit of career-oriented goals, and refuse to associate with those who are "beneath" them socially. Young marrieds agonize over how to spend their resources. Should they buy a boat or have a child? Climbing the money tree usually finds us sliding into the money pit of selfish choices.

Our thinking is diminished whenever it is focused solely on productivity. If everything is pressed through the grid of "How will this advance my earning potential?" Longer-range issues fade in importance. If all your behavior must fulfill standards of practicality—in other words, must bring you immediate rewards—you are creating self-limiting habits and patterns of thinking that will be hard to change. As the ruthless ax of productivity cuts away at inefficiency, its powerful rhythm may not stop to resist chopping into the soft wood of the meek and oppressed. Students who take only "practical" courses have already begun to swing the ax. They miss out on the enriching disciplines that make life more meaningful. As Os Guiness writes, we "have too much to live with, too little to live for." Even business majors would do well to be so "impractical" as to read poetry or learn how to reflect on personal experience and write about it. Not everything can be "productive" in measurable terms.

Dreams of affluence lure some people to financially rewarding jobs that they hate but feel trapped in because they have become dependent on the income. A wise friend once advised me against thrusting my hands into these Golden Handcuffs: "Always value job satisfaction more highly than financial return. Job satisfaction often compensates for modest pay, but high wages rarely counterbalance unhappiness on the job." When we hate our daily routine, the disgust takes its toll in ways that no number of fancy dinners will allow us to ignore.

Attempting to maintain even an appearance of wealth can become a destructive preoccupation. If most of our efforts go into producing sleek bodies in high fashion clothes, we are devaluating inner beauty, that muscle called character that can be "toned up" only through moral calisthenics. Similarly, the trouble with having a materialistic motivation for education is that a degree tends to be seen as nothing more than a "ticket" for something else, riches or higher status. As discussed in chapter 2, tickets are purchased, ripped in half, and discarded when the awaited event arrives. Education is far more than something to put on a résumé.

What will you sacrifice to live like a king or a queen? Not God's kingdom, I hope. If you remove your green-colored glasses, you may discover that the spy called materialism has infiltrated more deeply than you had suspected. Clear vision certainly aids the attack on the enemy.

Spies that Buzz and Whirr and Ding: Technology

Another subtle enemy of the thinking Christian is found in the sneaky undercover world of *technology*. This covert operation so pervades our society in dynamic yet oppressive ways that it has become the latest embodiment of the phrase, "You can't live with it and you can't live without it." We so love the latest gadget that we tend to accept—and buy—each new convenience without much thought. More and more people are literally captivated by such technological advancements as computers that can "think" or televisions that can project in three dimensions. The ranks of these uncritical worshipers of science are growing, engaging in an idolatry that Regent College professor James Houston has called "technolatry." Where does this love for "progress" lead?

An affinity for technology becomes an enemy of the mind when its values, such as speed and efficiency, dominate our choices. We may even begin to think of ourselves as technological units, anonymous bytes being processed in the mainframe of a computerized society, relegated to serve but not to create. Then we forget that what is admirable in a computer or microwave oven is not always a worthy human attribute. When speed and efficiency become a way of life, we begin to treat everything and everybody as a means to achieving *our* goals on *our* terms whenever it suits *our* convenience.

Speed becomes an enemy of the Christian mind whenever it perverts our view of time. If quicker is better, why bother to contemplate? If you are in a rush to get out of school and begin working, will you appreciate the present? If you are impatient with any circumstance that goes slowly, how can you ever be content? And yet, contemplation, appreciating the present (and the past), and contentment are all marks of a mind that is searching for truth and integrating knowledge toward that end. Wisdom is less likely to be in a hurry, because it knows where it is going and trusts God about getting there.

Efficiency is another technological value that, when overstated, will discourage kingdom-oriented thinking. When all activities are streamlined to reduce the friction factor, ethical and spiritual questions are rarely raised. How could you have an "efficient" meditation on the Scriptures? Is it a waste of time to cultivate a friendship that will make no contribution to your immediate goals?

When efficiency is the model, measurable results become the goal and we gauge success by performance alone. Because the second question we usually ask someone we have just met is "What do you do?" people tend to describe themselves in terms of their function: they are students or teachers or mechanics or entrepreneurs. A nation fixated on efficiency will honor the functions that seem to keep the machine of society running smoothly toward higher ground. How would Jesus be evaluated by this yardstick? In thirty years he made a few tables. In the next three he attracted a large following, lost his popularity, and then died.

Another consequence of an efficiency orientation is a complacent acceptance of transiency. It is often more efficient, in the short run, to use something once and then dispose of it. We use Kleenex instead of handkerchiefs and plastic communion cups instead of glass ones. We prefer cheap paperbacks to leather-bound books because we don't plan to reread them. As we become comfortable with disposing of *things* we find it difficult to persevere with ideas, emotions, and relationships. If there is trouble, we can simply move on and try the "new and improved model." Commitment to enduring truth is contrary to the spirit of a technological age.

In *I Believe in the Creator,* Houston comments that technology speeds up a system that is already too fast. Normally, "we think faster than we speak, speak faster than we act, and act faster than we have character to sustain." In other words, our capacity to act and speak and think is usually beyond the strength of our integrity. (Computers or not, I still need to count to ten to control my temper.) Since technology exacerbates this process, we should greet technological advancements as much with caution as with open arms.

Technology may serve to simplify your studying or writing, but it is a cruel master. Be wary of its spies, for their distractions can diminish your education as much as enhance it.

Spies That Pontificate with Chalk: Jell-O Mold Education

Perhaps the subtlest subversive in our midst is the *educational system itself.* How can this be so? How can you be told, on the one hand, to value education and take it seriously; and on the other, to be suspicious of smooth-talking "experts?" Just as there are different motives for going to college, there are different worldviews and educational philosophies, all calling for your allegiance. One particularly devilish part of the system is what I call the Great University Mold-Maker. Somehow, without any grand conspiracy, each college tends to turn out graduates who are strikingly similar in substance. You might say that they must have been poured into the same mold. They are so hard to tell apart.

How is a preformed college graduate created? Just as with a Jell-O mold, you start with the wiggly stuff itself: in this case, the quality of the students' high school education. In most cases, freshmen are quite malleable. If their previous schooling did little to make them discerning or wise, students' wobbly ideas will dissolve in a liquid labeled "openness to all ideas." The Mold-Makers can then add "fruit," that is, a wide variety of conflicting ideas, delivered on a platter of happy incongruities. Finally, the entire bland mixture goes into the refrigerator to cool off. In educational terms, students learn that passion ought not be wasted on defending any particular idea, because that idea might not be able to stand up to all the objections raised against it. The result is a delightfully cool, and largely substance-free conformity. "Quality control" virtually assures that all servings are identical.

When indiscriminate pluralism is its intent, the educational process can be an enemy to the thinking Christian.

Even after this supposedly enlightening, sharpening experience, you can end up as a jiggly blob. Jesus said he came not to bring peace, "but a sword" (Matt. 10:34). What can you cut with a spoonful of Jell-O? Dull experiences in the classroom will drain inspiration from the most dedicated student, yet too few teachers have resisted the trend toward dreary homogeneity. After mental and spiritual battles against all sorts of foes, the dream to transform students' lives dies, replaced by a sense that "doing one's job" means "keeping them occupied" or "stirring no controversy." The student becomes a casualty. I'll freely admit that some of what I learned in school was as much an obstacle as a help. How can students learn to value truth when questions in the classroom are not solicited or new ideas not taken seriously? How can they learn to care when the system itself conspires against caring?

Not only can education be thought of or carried out improperly, it can also be overstated. Even in a book that has set out to encourage the educational experience, it must be acknowledged that education is not a panacea. It will not solve all your problems or reform the wickedness in human hearts. Education can be a wondrous adventure, but only with God's grace will it open our hearts to truth. Students need the Savior no less than business managers, or construction workers, or . . . professors.

Zoological Guidance

Jesus has succinctly condensed the advice of this chapter into one pithy phrase: "I am sending you out like sheep among wolves. Therefore be as shrewd as snakes and as innocent as doves" (Matt. 10:16). In this verse, Jesus recognizes at least three realities. First, the world is not a friendly place. He does not say, "I send you out as diners into a smorgasbord," or even "as athletes into the Olympics." We are, by immediate appearances, at a significant disadvantage. I would rather be a lion among the wolves, but lamb I am.

Second, taking this circumstance to heart, we are protected by putting on the serpent's shrewdness and the dove's innocence. As snake, we are wily, tough-minded, and discerning, not easily fooled. As dove, we are morally pure, sensitive to subtle goodness, alert to the presence of God. A snake is a symbol of cunning and therefore knows the weaknesses of the enemy. A dove is a symbol of peace and offers love through an olive branch of forgiveness.

Since either of these traits on their own would be useful in a society of wolves, Jesus' third point is somewhat surprising. His disciples are to hold these qualities *simultaneously*, and to do otherwise would be to miss the blessing. Innocence without shrewdness would make me naive, guileless but gullible, an easy though blame-free prey for the wolves. If I were only shrewd, I would be cynical or bombastic, resistant to the wolves' wiles, but nonetheless becoming like them because I would imitate their tactics and ignore the state of my soul. However, if I *combine* innocence and shrewdness, I can be awestruck by God's simplest wonder without being naive, and I can be a careful analyst without being cynical.

A shrewd innocence, though filled with childlike wonder at every beautiful discovery, is not impressed by evil. An innocent shrewdness, though able to spot and respond to error, can also spot and appreciate the contributions of others. In short, those who follow both serpent and dove become wise, able to coil or slither, fly or coo, as the need arises.

Such are the characteristics of anyone who would oppose the enemies of the thinking Christian. The first group of enemies mentioned in this chapter (pride, cynicism, and fear) might be called sins against innocence. They attack thinkers by making them feel that moral purity and childlike wonder are beneath their dignity, that innocence is silly, juvenile, and unrealistic. The second group of enemies (materialism, technology, and pre-packaged education) might be called sins against shrewdness. They attack thinkers by calling discernment judgmental, harsh, and intolerant. Being a chameleon among wolves won't do. But Christians with both innocence and shrewdness can brave the evils of the world, trusting the Lamb of God for safe passage. Such is the life of those who would love God with their minds.

What's in Your Heart?

1. If, as Chesterton says, a thinking person "should always attack the strongest thing in his own time," what should we be attacking today?
2. Of pride, cynicism, and fear, which "enemy from within" do you struggle with most? Why? Which one do you most notice in others?
3. How have materialism, technology, and education influenced your heart for truth? If you think you have not been influenced, consider this: Would you rather have a "normal" amount of money and techno-gadgets or a mind that truly loves God? Which do you presently spend more effort acquiring?

Not to Worry: The God of Creation Is Also Lord over Karl Marx's World

Christianity is not so much a leap in
the dark as it is a stab in the light.
J. I. Packer

In grade school, I learned what it
meant to have the world by the tail. At
recess, we played crack-the-whip, an out-
door death wish in which a line of hand-
holding fourth-graders ran in serpentine
fashion at full speed. As the line doubled
back, the whip "cracked," and we kids
would receive about 20 "G"s of force, sending the whippers and whippees into various
contortions never designed for the human
body. We called this fun. Since I was the
smallest fourth-grader, I was usually put at
the end of the line so that when the whip

cracked, I would be sent sailing parallel to the ground, knocking over innocent bystanders like so many bowling pins. Having the world by the tail is not all it's cracked up to be.

My world has sent me flailing about many times, sometimes due to confrontational assertions such as: "According to Ayn Rand's novel *Fountainhead,* Christianity is too self-denying." Or, "Marxists show that Christians have always oppressed the lower class." Or, "B. F. Skinner's reward-and-punishment scheme makes Christian ethics obsolete." Or, "After I read *Understanding Media,* I could no longer make sense of God." I have personally heard all these arguments. As I have struggled to reply to them, the most important guideline has been this: To some degree, each position has its merits. Wait a minute—did I say that? How could any conscientious apologist for Christianity admit such a thing?

At stake in our response to any formidable challenge to the gospel is not only our defense of the faith but our integrity about the truth. What do we do when we find sound reasoning in a non-Christian view? Although some of these arguments won't trouble us (they may even enlighten us), others may significantly disturb our beliefs. There *are* certain risks to having a heart for truth. Socrates said that the unexamined life is not worth living. True enough, but the examined life is not exactly all crumpets and caviar.

Howard Jones wrote a clever article nearly fifty years ago called "The Attractions of Stupidity." In it, he suggests that the easiest, least challenging way to survive in school is to stay loyal to the unexamined life. Most students, he says, are attracted to this form of "stupidity." They strive to blend in with their peers, to be undistinguished, to follow the prevailing winds of thought and practice, to borrow unexamined thoughts from others like the Romans did, to be, in a word: conformist. This bland approach is appealing, according to Jones, because conformists are usually quite successful. Those who accept fashionable values without question tend to "get on in life."

Some, however, eschew the ranks of the Romans and gravitate instead toward the Greeks. They seek not so much to borrow from others as to master what is in their own intellectual orbit. This sort of mind, says Jones, is willing to relinquish opinions proved to be false: "It is humble before the vast ocean of ignorance, and modest in respect to its own minute attainments. It allows a considerable margin for the possibility of being self-deceived." He also warns those who would take the Greek approach that—though the life of the real thinker is exciting and interesting—it can also be "an uncertain, an uncomfortable, possibly an inglorious . . . career."

When we take the jump toward developing a heart for truth, we may feel at times as if we were merely falling, uncertain of the kind of landing we might make. For example, with very little background in psychology, I once took a course taught by one of the most published researchers in behavioral marital therapy, a sophisticated theory of learning based on rewards. Immediately, the course content left the realm of "information to know for an exam" and leaped to the status of "a philosophy to explain all of human experience." Since I held that *Christianity* explained human experience, the compelling aspects of this system's explanation gave my faith an earthquake, and "Dr. Richter" was not about to let up on the aftershocks.

One temptation in such a situation is to say, "Those arrogant behaviorists, who do they think they are, rejecting the Lord and Sustainer of life?" Too often, I think, we Christians refuse even to consider any common ground between our "philosophy" and alternative belief systems. Like a good conformist, do you simply go about the business of passing your courses? What you may not realize is that, by dismissing other ideas wholesale, you also dismiss any truth that may lie within them. It is more honest *and* enlightening to investigate the challenge of the new perspective, comparing what you are learning with what you know to be true in Christ Jesus. This approach inevitably leads to any number of questions, including these two types: questions that cannot be easily answered by appealing directly to Scripture and questions that cause genuine doubts.

So, for example, you may discover the first type of question in a course on contemporary moral problems if you are asked to develop ethical guidelines for the issue of surrogate mothering. Or, in Mass Communication, if the assignment is to write about your thoughtful response to technology. Or, in Latin American Studies, if you must take a position about liberation theology. What do you do? Jesus didn't talk about AIDS or television or nuclear warheads or Marxist priests or smog. Does God care about these issues? If so, how do we discern his wisdom?

You may discover the second type of question when you hear the feminist critique of Western history and are struck by male injustice toward women. In Biology 101, the professor may ably defend a form of evolution that does not mesh with the interpretation of Genesis you've been taught previously. The Modern Poetry course that your Christian friend recommended may become a swamp of intellectual quicksand, sucking you ever deeper into the torment of despair and pessimism. What do you do? Do you revert to being a private, only-my-best-friend-knows type of Christian, a person who keeps God in a tidy box, opened only on Sundays? That question is not as simple as it sounds, because taking God out of the box means you risk having your image of him challenged, changed, or diminished. But might you also see a larger, less-confined God? Might you discover that, as J. B. Phillips's title asserts, *Your God Is Too Small?* At any rate, you will almost certainly suffer doubt and need to cope with the anxiety of pondering an age-old dilemma: What is truth?

These, then, seem to be the two central challenges for the thinking Christian: answering questions about which the Bible appears to be silent and dealing with doubt, when God himself seems to be silent. Before examining these two issues, remember that you have good cause for courage. When the disciples were faced with difficulties, Jesus told them, "In this world you will have trouble. But take heart! I have overcome the world" (John 16:33). In contemporary language, he might have said, "Not to worry; the God of Creation is also the Lord over Karl Marx."

When God's Word Seems to Be Silent

In a Mass Communication class, the relevance of the Scriptures can be an elusive concept. Sometimes I get students thinking about their method of applying biblical ideals to our world by asking a series of questions.

"Do you think that television is one of the most powerful forces in the world today?"

"Yes."

"Does the Bible say anything about television?"

"No."

"So, does that mean that God has nothing to say about one of the most powerful forces in the world today?"

"Uhm . . . well . . . isn't there a verse about Samson breaking a cable?"

Though we often pound the pulpit about God's sovereignty, we may find ourselves in the position of saying that he is master of the universe but not of the living room. This limited view of God is usually the result of theological mixed messages about the nature of life and the nature of the Scriptures.

As mentioned briefly in chapter 11, one of the most common errors in the history of the church has been to divide life into two distinct categories marked "spiritual" and "secular." We put our experiences into separate boxes, and never the twain shall meet. Whereas the spiritual box gets filled with obviously religious activities such as prayer, Bible study, evangelism, and church going, the secular box gets filled with homework, cars, dates, and movie going, essentially everything else. In so doing, no matter how much we say otherwise, we are denying God's authority over how we spend *most* of our time.

I've heard of a sign in a church that says, "Divine service is conducted here four times daily." The slogan was posted not on a church marquee but above a kitchen sink. If, in fact, the dishwashers adopted the attitude of the phrase, they would be following Paul's admonition, "Whatever you do, work at it with all your heart, as working for the Lord, not for men" (Col. 3:23). The call in Scripture is not to a set of "religious" duties but to a life with God—a life in the Spirit. As we begin to be transformed into Christ's likeness, we see that all of life is under his lordship, that no part of our lives is outside "the sacred canopy," that even the most ordinary tasks, such as brushing one's teeth or doing a term paper, can be understood as part of our life with him.

The way to resolve the tension between "sacred" and "secular" is not to fill the spiritual box with so much church-related busy-ness that the other box is almost empty. That would be saying that the person involved in the greatest number of obviously religious activities would be the most holy. That sounds a bit like the Pharisees—and you know what Jesus said about them!

Instead, the idea is to have only *one* box, the one marked "spiritual." Into it we put *all* of life: theology, prayer, and Scripture memory cards, but also our studies or careers, our treatment of the earth, and even our peanut butter sandwiches. Along the way we recognize that if God's kingdom extends to our intellectual life, it must also be relevant to the ideas and problems that perplex the thinking Christian. In principle, then, we accept the view that all truth is God's truth and that no question is beyond his concern. If, as novelist Charles Williams said, "Everything natural is supernatural and everything supernatural is natural," then the natural, secular, ordinary world of Karl Marx and Jack London and Gloria Steinem must be God's world, too. This doesn't make everything that they wrote true, but it does assure us that we are not outside of God's domain when we read writers who challenge the Christian view. Surely God is not threatened by contrary opinions!

The Christian life is circumscribed by our worldview and also by the way in which we apply the Scriptures. During the Reformation, one of the issues of contention within the church was how to use the Scripture in moral decision making. The following abbreviated (and, I hope, not misrepresented) versions of this debate are relevant to our discussion. One group said that "whatever is not overtly forbidden is permitted," and the other group said that "whatever is not overtly permitted is forbidden." On the surface, each perspective resonates with an accepted principle of the Christian life. The first focuses on freedom, the second on holiness. When taken to the extreme, both views become problematic. If I apply the "not overtly forbidden" guide, I could conclude that drug experimentation, X-rated phone calls, and smog-belching cars are all "permissible." If I apply the "not overtly permitted" perspective, I might wonder if I could use electricity, go see *Dumbo,* or avail myself of the latest medical advances. The problem with both guidelines is that they look to the Bible for a *direct* word about every important situation in life, a method of application called "proof-texting."

Must we find a verse that speaks exactly to every possible moral question? Even if we do, are we certain that we know God's mind just because one verse addresses our question (or seems to)? The answer to both is "no." For anyone to survive as a thinking Christian, God's Word needs to be seen not as a Rolodex file from which we may snatch individual verses as we choose, but as a revelation of God's character and purpose. Since the Bible is a reflection of the person of God, behind even the most culture-bound command is a principle that speaks timelessly. As we seek his wisdom about issues not directly addressed in the Bible, we can be confident that the theology derived from Scripture will speak to that issue in some way.

For purposes of illustration, we could reclaim the issue that began this section. What does the Bible have to say about things such as sitcoms and ads for soda pop? There are many places to go for help with the faith issues related to the sticky problem of television viewing. One possibility is to choose a reference centered on stewardship, which is promoted in Genesis (1:26–31; 2:15). Should we not be good managers of our time, and therefore our time in front of the TV? Or, in the Ten Commandments, we see principles that are regularly disregarded on most television programs. Garrison Keillor once defined a soap opera as a show in which rich people in nice cars break the Ten Commandments, starting from number ten and working backward. Perhaps we could also look to connections between Jesus' teaching on contentment and the hundreds of times we have heard "Buy this now! It's new and improved!" in TV's incessant commercials.

Although many texts are applicable, one passage that can inform our thinking about the extra-biblical issue of television viewing is Paul's perspective in 1 Corinthians 6:12–20. Speaking in the context of abuses in the Corinthian church, from lawsuits within the church to sex with prostitutes, Paul appeals to a principle regarding the Christian's relationship to moral law. He says, "Everything is permissible for me—but not everything is beneficial. 'Everything is permissible for me'—but I will not be mastered by anything" (v. 12). Or, as the Phillips version puts it: "As a Christian I may do anything, but that does not mean that everything is good for me. I may do everything, but I must not be a slave of anything."

In this statement, Paul argues that Christian freedom has its limits. In the Corinthians' case, they were so busy saying "Hooray for grace" that they said hooray all the way to the red-light district. Paul's response is "Just because in some sense, every*thing* is neutral, that doesn't mean we are neutral."

Because we have been bought with a price, we are the Lord's and must treat our body as a holy vessel that is affected by whatever we pour into it. Therefore, two guidelines must inform our every action, from sex with prostitutes to watching television. First, our freedom should be restricted to behavior that is edifying or "beneficial." I may be "free" to watch TV, but that doesn't make TV edifying. I should be careful about shows that titillate or exploit my baser instincts, shows that lead me to deny the fruit of the Spirit or commend unbiblical values. I should be careful that my sense of freedom does not make me susceptible to the latest lie in the latest commercial. Second, our freedom should be restricted to behavior over which we can exercise control. Paul says not to be *mastered* by anything. How much of our TV viewing is compulsive? We are not in control if we are media-sponges who mindlessly absorb any and all images on the flickering screen. As we read about the Corinthians, we may be shocked about the prostitutes; but we sure happily watch a lot of them on the tube.

Strictly speaking, I am not trying to build a case for or against television viewing, though the subject *is* neglected by the church. My point is that Scripture does speak to contemporary issues, though we may have to do a bit of searching to uncover its wisdom. Since the Bible is the reliable Word of God, the effort is worth it.

When God Seems to Be Silent

What if your investigations produce more questions than answers and you are more wracked by doubt than when you began? Sometimes even diligent Bible study can leave you wondering what God's Word is really saying. Furthermore, the more you learn about world civilization and church history, the more you may be confused about the validity of your faith. For example, you may discover troubling parallels between Old Testament narratives and Near Eastern myths. Your professor might propose that Korean War brainwashing techniques are akin to many evangelistic practices. These tensions are not easily resolved.

How can you deal with the gnawing in your soul, the hunger that won't be satisfied? College can be a dreary tennis match of conflicting opinions, where one thought pops over the net and is returned as a counterbalancing idea, which leads to still another. Back and forth the volley goes, with no idea ever clearly the winner. "On the one hand" always leads to "on the other hand" until you've run out of hands. What if your roommate with the 4.0 grade point average says that Jesus is the weakest solution ever offered humankind—suited only for nitwits who ignore reality? You almost believe him, at least for the moment since you agree on some compelling evidence. Your brain becomes a battleground with little gray-cell casualties getting in the way of making any progress toward truth.

Doubt. It is a nagging, life-sucking dread that immobilizes and agonizes the soul. But it is also an inspiring catalyst toward life that motivates and stimulates. Which is true? I suppose it depends on which side of doubt you find yourself. You may be glad to reap the benefits of having walked through the darkness, but the walk itself you would prefer to avoid. One thing is certain in the life of faith, especially for those who take the mind seriously: doubt is inevitable. But it is also not a sin. In fact, it may be an indication that your faith is growing.

Essayist and novelist Frederick Buechner writes, "Whether your faith is that there is a God or that there is not a God, if you don't have any doubts you are either kidding yourself or asleep. Doubts are the ants in the pants of faith. They keep it alive and moving." Buechner reasons that in all of life there is some measure of *faith*. In everything that we take by faith, there is a lack of absolute certainty.

And, where we are unsure, we will doubt. In fact, one could argue that the more we stretch our faith, the more doubt we will encounter. So the person utterly without doubt is probably someone with little faith as well.

The reassuring part of this deduction is that doubt is part of the human condition, not something that afflicts only Christians. Everyone doubts. However, because some beliefs are challenged more often than others, some people are given more opportunity to doubt. Some beliefs, such as the validity of astrology or the idea that anyone can become president, are so popular or innocuous that they receive little attention. Just because roommates or professors call our faith into question does not make the object of our faith less likely to be true—but if we are on the receiving end of many troubling questions, the inquiry can create considerable internal pain and external controversy.

Neither does the existence of doubt mean that the object of doubt is untrue. For example, although most of medieval Europe doubted that the world was round, their hunch did not make the earth flat. Doubt can obscure our vision of reality, but if disbelief made a position false, all the doubted things in the world would cease to be true. (Didn't people once doubt that disease was caused by unseen living organisms?) Despite this assurance, sometimes we are so bombarded by questions that we think the structure of our faith will come crashing down. Although "faith" is partly our own personal experience, it is also a set of presuppositions that is fortified by philosophical and physical evidence. If it is both personal *and* objective, no amount of argumentative shelling will destroy its foundations. We can be confident that the truth will win out, or especially since so many bombs are either duds or easily de-activated.

Doubt is not a statement of unbelief. In his excellent book on faith struggles, *In Two Minds,* Os Guinness takes to task the notion that doubt is the opposite of faith. He writes, "To believe is to be 'in one mind' about accepting something as true; to disbelieve is to be 'in one mind' about rejecting it. To doubt is to waver between the two, to believe and disbelieve at once and so to be 'in two minds.'" Too often we feel that our doubt is a failure of faith, an admission that "I must be a terrible Christian if I doubt so much." Although being "in two minds" may not be pleasant, it does not deserve the intensity of this accusation.

The Scriptures tell us that we are in good company if we struggle with uncertainties. Abraham was not really sure about God's promises until his son Isaac was born. Moses, Isaiah, and Jeremiah were skeptical of God's choosing them as his spokesmen. Thomas, the Duke of Doubt, had to touch our Lord's hands and feet to confirm his resurrection. Even John the Baptist had doubts. When he was in prison, not too long before he was beheaded, he sent his disciples to Jesus with a question: "Are you the one who was to come, or should we expect someone else?" (Matt. 11:3). Even more amazing is Jesus' response. Did he get depressed or angry and say, "Way to go, John. You of all people should have no doubts!" No, after Jesus pointed to evidence of his own messiahship, he commended John to the crowd: "Among those born of women there has not risen anyone greater than John the Baptist" (v. 11a). Because Jesus and his mission could not be toppled by John's uncertainty, he was no more distraught over John's concerns than I am when my daughters worry that monsters will get them as they sleep. I *know* there are no goblins in their rooms. (I've locked them all in my closet!)

Though doubt is not necessarily sinful, it is not entirely blissful either. John's agony was real, and so are my daughters' fears. What some have called the "dark night of the soul" or "the absence of God" can lead to many sleepless nights. Just as my daughters want reassurance from me and relief from their nightmares, so do we want God to heal and comfort us. Yet, because *thinking* Christians will always have questions, some of them unanswerable in the present age, our security lies in trusting the Lord and believing that these issues will ultimately be resolved.

While we should not fear our doubts or feel guilty because of them neither should we take pride in them, as if somehow the more doubtful we are, the more integrity we have about discovering the complexity of truth. As Martin Luther said, "The Holy Spirit is not a skeptic." This side of heaven "we see but a poor reflection" (1 Cor. 13:12), though we should strive to see as clearly as we can. One day, the day that lasts forever, we will see through the glass clearly and understand the truth because then we will gaze directly into the face of Jesus Christ.

Since it is toward that end that even doubt moves us, one could say that doubt has a useful purpose. Just as Jesus' faith was challenged before he began his ministry, so our faith must be tested if it is to mature. When we doubt, we will be tempted to forsake elements of our beliefs or pledge our faith blindly and repress our questions. Neither action offers much of a solution. Since all of life requires faith of some sort, there is no escape from the anxiety of doubt. As Guinness says, "There is no faith which cannot choose to cast doubt on some other faith." The best response to inner doubt or critical inquiry is to address the issues to the best of our ability and piety. Though thinking may unearth certain challenges to one's faith, it also serves faith by working toward an answer, or at least a negotiated settlement.

By taking your doubts seriously, you can incur a number of benefits. You may so convincingly resolve a particular doubt that on the next go-around, the question arouses little or no anxiety. You may, in searching for an answer, discover more about God's ways, grow in spiritual and theological maturity, and learn how to hold on to a complex of issues without having everything resolved. You may discover that the doubt alerted you to error, that your belief was tainted or misplaced. As we experience the trustworthiness of God in the midst of the inquisition, our faith increases. As my daughter Laura learns to trust me, she will no longer say, "Don't drop me," when I lift her over my head. Her faith in "Daddy," tested every time I toss her around, will grow confident and secure. So, too, our faith will grow as we are "raised" by our heavenly Father.

You have not been the first to question or wonder or endure intellectual and spiritual torment, nor will you be the last. But you can find solace in the midst of your trials. As reassurance to the Jews after their seemingly aimless struggle in the desert for forty years, Moses addressed the purpose of their wanderings:

> Remember how the LORD your God led you all the way in the desert these forty years, to humble you and to test you in order to know what was in your heart, whether or not you would keep his commands. He humbled you, causing you to hunger and then feeding you with manna, which neither you nor your fathers had known, to teach you that man does not live on bread alone but on every word that comes from the mouth of the LORD. Your clothes did not wear out and your feet did not swell during these forty years. Know then in your heart that as a man disciplines his son, so the LORD your God disciplines you (Deut. 8:2–5).

When God seems silent, the Scriptures speak of his presence. When we cannot sense this presence, we can trust that God is indeed at work in our behalf—testing us to make our faith stronger, disciplining us to make us spiritually complete. Of one remarkable, gracious truth we may be sure: The Lord wants to know us even more than we want to know him. He wants to remake us into his image even more than we want to be remade. When I see the magnitude of God's love, I can trust him for the smaller issues. Although I don't know what will happen to the generations of people who never heard of Christ, I *trust* that God is a perfect union of justice and mercy and will do what is right and loving. When I see him face to face, I know I will find his decisions heavenly and his presence glorious.

What's in Your Heart?

1. Take a nonbiblical contemporary issue such as nuclear weapons, terrorism, or children's advertising and work toward discovering some biblical insight that informs the topic.
2. "Everyone doubts." Explore various ways to apply this phrase. What causes you the most doubt?
3. What most reaffirms your faith during periods of intense doubt?

14   Seeing a Penny and Hearing a Bell

There is always Music amongst the trees in the Garden, but our hearts must be very quiet to hear it.

Minnie Aumonier

A professor once told me: "A liberal arts education not only helps you learn how to make a living, it teaches you how to live." Although the statement may overstate the power of the liberal arts, it does point to the idea that a true education is not something that you submit to for four years and then ignore as you move on. Education is not something that is done *to* you, as if all you had to do was find the hinge on your skull, open up, and let the information pour in. Neither does this "spectator" perspective work when it comes to reading a book called *A Heart for Truth*. Acquiring wisdom from a blackboard, a laboratory, or a book requires your active participation and personal commitment. A heart for truth either transcends the machinations of memorizing data or it is not present at all.

In chapter 2, I implied that this "heart" was like our sense of touch. I said that a heart for truth was a *feel* for the texture of truth, an awareness of the way knowledge loops together into one seamless tapestry that leads to the Master Weaver himself. As with the upcoming chapter on study habits, I'd like to add to this "sense of touch" the sense of sight and hearing.

First, *sight*. In *Pilgrim at Tinker Creek,* Annie Dillard tells the story of how, when she was six or seven years of age, she would hide pennies in various sidewalk or tree cracks. With great joy, she would imagine how excited some passer-by would be when a penny was discovered. In this image, Dillard offers a unique perspective toward daily experience: There are pennies everywhere if only we have eyes to see. She writes:

> The world is fairly studded and strewn about with pennies cast broadside from a generous hand. But—and this is the point—who gets excited by a mere penny? . . . It is dire poverty indeed when a man is so malnourished and fatigued that he won't stoop to pick up a penny. But if you cultivate a healthy poverty and simplicity, so that finding a penny will literally make your day, then, since the world is in fact planted in pennies, you have with your poverty bought a lifetime of days.

One test of a mind that loves God is this kind of sight. More than book-learning, more than grades, more than a diploma, a heart for truth sees in the world a wealth of pennies. You may not make the honor roll, go on to graduate school, or reach your career goals, but if you seek to *know*—if you look with your head and heart and put your hands to work with what you know—you will discover that the joy of learning will guide you to new revelations like a map to buried treasure. A person thus primed is always alert to the pennies in the cracks that are waiting to be plucked.

Second, *hearing.* A spirit of keen searching is partly what Jesus called for when he said, "He who has ears, let him hear" (Matt. 13:9). Of course, we all have ears, but we do not all hear in the same way. Some people listen to find fault; others only attend to what is entertaining. But Jesus encouraged his disciples to listen with a ready responsiveness, an eagerness to understand and follow. Since the ear can be trained one way or the other, how we *listen* partly determines what we actually *hear.* To an engineer, noisy rush-hour traffic may be cacophony; to a composer, a symphony. How do you interpret the sounds around you?

In 1623, when he had been sick for several months, John Donne wrote a series of devotions that addressed many issues related to suffering. In Donne's day, the local church bell would ring in a certain way whenever there was a death in the parish. As you might imagine, on hearing the bell, people would ask each other who had died. To this oft-asked question, Donne replied, ". . . never send to know for whom the bell tolls; it tolls for thee." His point was that since "no man is an island," we are all affected by any loss to the community, and all deaths are our concern. The tolling of the bell is never unrelated to us.

Lest you think me morbid or uncouth to end this book with a discussion of death, I'd like to direct your attention to the bell. Not only did Donne wish his readers to contemplate the interrelatedness of human society, he wanted them to see that many events in the world pertain to us, even when we think they primarily affect others. So you might ask: "What messages am I missing? What bells am I not hearing? How does a heart for truth sharpen my listening ability?"

Some educational chimes are so consistent that they are often overlooked. When "the bell tolls"—that is, when class begins each day or when a question is asked or new ideas are presented—you might well remember Donne's words. Then say, "Never send to know for whom the school bell tolls. This day's class or that question or new idea is meant for me. It is not for the purposes of note-taking, exam-cramming and grade-making. It is for *my* hearing ears and *my* life." What better time to begin listening than now, when the wisdom bell will ring so often?

Whenever students begin to see the wealth of pennies before them or hear the bells of truth pealing wherever they turn, their exhilaration is contagious. Suddenly knowledge is alive with meaning. The Bible is no longer a boring Sunday school book, reading lists are more than assignments, and nature becomes an ever-present teacher. If this awakening does not happen until the senior year, students are pleased and saddened at the same time. They wonder why they waited so long to set their eyes to seeing and their ears to hearing and what riches they missed for being blind and deaf so long.

What creates the vision for seeing pennies and the con-centration for hearing bells? There is something about the "heart for truth" that makes it more alive to experience. I suppose this is really a mystery, since we cannot make "aha" moments happen. Not every time we strain our eyes or ears will we be rewarded. Even so, says the writer of Proverbs, we are to turn our ears to wisdom and apply our hearts to understanding (see Prov. 2:2).

One irony in this "bell" metaphor is that the transition from high school to college usually means a decrease in the number of literal bells. Consequently, whatever ringing you hear in college is significantly dependent on the quality of your own hearing. Some students never ask for whom the bell tolls because they do not hear it ringing. Yet, as the Spirit moves, the bell will send a signal, however faint. In the midst of many distractions, try to be quick and listen hard for it. If you seek it when you wrestle with "the angelic beast in the mirror," you will discover what it means to see the fullness of redemption in your life. Listen for it in your relationships, as you consider how best to be with "those whom you love." Search after the sound of the bell as you mature as an "intellectual (!) Christian." And when you find a bell, ring it as long and loud as you can.

As you take your faith to college and open your heart to truth, the pennies you see and the bells you hear will begin to multiply, leading you ever more directly to the Father, who is the Source of truth; to the Son, who is the Incarnation of truth; and to the Holy Spirit, who is the Revealer of truth.

Two Postscripts

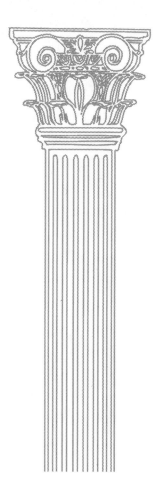

*Writing for Dr. Pagan**

A strong foe is better than a weak
friend.

Edward Dahlberg

Ulysses fought Cyclops. Jesus endured
the treachery of Judas. Some of you will
meet your Professor Moriarty in the smirk
of Dr. Pagan. Though we would be foolish to think of all non-Christian professors
in adversarial terms, most secular campuses
have an infamous God-buster atheist who
delights in troubling tender souls.

Suppose your Dr. Pagan assigns an
open-ended writing project, "Complete a
research paper on a topic of your choice
pertinent to the course." What would you
do? Your options include: read *Cliff Notes*
on three books and synthesize what you
don't know about them; buy a term paper
through the service agency Plagiarists

*Adapted from material originally published in *Student
Leadership Journal,* Fall 1990, pp. 18–19.

213

Anonymous; find the safest, dullest topic and write a supremely boring paper; or seek to have your Christian faith inform your topic with intelligence, witness, insight, wit, and integrity.

All right, I stacked the deck. But the last option *is* intriguing. At any secular school, when writing for Dr. Pagan, Dr. Agnostic, or Dr. I-Haven't-Got-a-Clue, you might find yourself leaning toward the adventure of writing a paper from a Christian perspective for a professor without a Christian perspective. How do you write this daring enterprise of insight, wit, and integrity?

Define Your Ultimate Purpose

First, consider what you want most out of this paper: an "A," a scalp, a jewel in your crown, or a genuine meeting of the minds. "That's easy," you say, "I want to evangelize my professor." If that's the case, you are already in trouble. Evangelizing is a worthy task; but, as a primary purpose, it usually leads to the evangelizer treating the evangelizee as a means to an end. For example, one student I know slips a Bible tract inside his term papers. On the outside, the tract looks like a $10 bill. Once opened, it reads, "Want something precious? Try Jesus!" Usually, the recipient would rather have the $10.

Instead, your purpose in the classroom can be seen within part of a larger claim on your life: to love God and to love your neighbor as yourself. How do you go about loving God when writing a term paper? Loving God means, among other things, imitating the way Jesus thinks—loving the truth, his truth, and working to discover it. Therefore, loving God means developing a biblical perspective about all areas of life, not just "theological" matters. If you catch the vision of learning as a way to love God by loving his truth, your papers are always important, irrespective of your professor's response. In fact, you will likely discover that the "unconverted" professor has some truth to teach you. A Biology professor may show you more to appreciate in the creation. An English teacher may lead you to insight about human nature through great literature.

The second part of "the greatest commandment" is to love your neighbor as yourself. If you want your professors and peers to be set free by the truth (even as you have been set free), decide what truth you most want to communicate and then how it could best be communicated in your present assignment.

You don't have to elaborate on a comprehensive four-point gospel every time you set out to express ideas. Although the task of writing an essay falls under the lordship of Christ, each paper does not need to have an explicitly evangelistic bent. Rather, your job is to analyze your topic truthfully and well. If carpenters set evangelism as their goal, rather than good craftsmanship and honest dealings, they might be more concerned about writing "Jesus Saves" on 2 by 4s than about nailing them properly. The phrase would be exposed when the house collapsed, but the homeowner will have missed the point.

Consider Dr. Pagan's Perspective

The simplest question is sometimes missed. Would *you* like your paper if *you* were Dr. Pagan? People who love their neighbors well do not love everyone in the same way; they love others the way others like to have love expressed to them. Answering the following questions will help you write in ways that will communicate a respectful and caring attitude toward your professors.

First, what do university professors like? They like work that is well organized, perceptive, creative, neat, ably documented, mechanically correct, clever, rigorously argued, and prompt. Whew! The point is that professors like good work. Weaving a Christian perspective into a poorly constructed paper doesn't make it a good paper. Be wary of claiming martyrdom when you receive a "D." What you may take as "being a fool for Christ" may be only being foolish.

Professors also enjoy students who have a passion for the issues discussed in class. One prof remarked to me that only one student in her course treated the assigned "position papers" as a true discussion of belief. The others were obediently fulfilling an assignment, but with little personal commitment.

Second, what do professors dislike? Besides poor work, they dislike clichéd answers to genuine questions, Christian jargon, and arrogant, holier-than-thou young twits telling them that their ideas are idiotic. Although professors may themselves act like arrogant, brainier-than-thou older twits, they still need to be approached with sensitivity.

Third, what do you know about this particular professor's view of Christianity? What pet peeves or commonalities are you aware of? Agree where you can and build bridges to more direct Christian thought. For example, "Nietzsche's candor about religion was and is refreshing, but his alternative offers little real hope."

Some professors, although they aren't sure about Christian ideas themselves, may simply be parroting the unreflective view around them that Christians are irrational, moralistic, and dull. Consider what you can do to demonstrate the intellectual defensibility, moral integrity, and fascinating appeal of the faith.

Choose Topics That Lend Themselves to Creative, Biblical Connections

Certain ideas bring to bear one's worldview with greater intensity than others. What topics would permit you to investigate and quote Christians in support of your thesis? How about a paper on C. S. Lewis's view of ethics in *Out of the Silent Planet*? Where possible, quote contemporary Christian thinkers on social issues.

Also, when given the option of choosing any person or social movement in a certain time period, you can usually find an outstanding Christian to do the talking for you. Examples include Pascal as an apologist during the Enlightenment, Jonathan Edwards for his impact during the colonial era, William Wilberforce as abolitionist in England, or Flannery O'Connor as a modern novelist.

Resources abound. Many publishing houses print books that integrate biblical theology and various fields of study. One book in particular, *Discipleship of the Mind* by James W. Sire, contains an extensive bibliography sorted by subject. You might also consult intellectually oriented Christians in your area—campus staff workers, pastors, or faculty—and most professors could point you toward influential Christians during a particular era.

Craft Your Arguments Wisely

Dr. Pagan is not a moron. You may confidently present a simple, convincing defense of a Christian position to your younger brother in fourth grade, but saying "Jesus loves you" to the prof who wrote his dissertation on "The Relationship between Protestantism and the Decline of Western Europe" will prove inadequate. Following a few guidelines may increase your survival rate.

Do your homework. The Holy Spirit is unlikely to generate spontaneous knowledge of St. Anselm's defense of God in your brain. If God is not usually in the business of taking things away—your car's sick carburetor, for example—neither is he in the business of implanting things instantly within, such as the outline of Calvin's *Institutes.* Though the Holy Spirit does reveal knowledge to us, it is sometimes through the dustiest book on the tallest shelf on the fourth floor of the east wing of the library. You must suffer through the mundane aspects of education like everyone else.

Study Christian resources. Determine what biblical principles or passages in Scripture might inform your topic. As you research your subject matter, you may discover that your library has many publications that speak from a Christian perspective. Much of this kind of learning can also take place as you talk with others about your projects.

State in Christian terms only what is pertinent to the essay. In a Small-Group Communication class, one student wrote a paper about leadership. In the first paragraph, without making any connection to the topic, the student wrote, "Oh, by the way, I am a follower of Jesus Christ." If not essential to the topic, such phrases are about as appropriate as, "Oh, by the way, I collect paper clips."

Restate Christian vocabulary in nontheological terms. Professors who balk at "we are wretched sinners bound for hell," might appreciate "we are constitutionally flawed and cannot be pure in motive or deed." Don't compromise your beliefs, but be flexible. Become "all things to all men" (1 Cor. 9:22).

Be honest about difficult areas. Christians are often prone to overstate their case. Why say "Christians make better lovers" when you can't prove that every pastor is a good kisser? If you are unsure, say so. There is nothing more boring (or frustrating) than a debate with a dogmatic, unyielding know-it-all. If you are forthright with your doubts, your professors may be more open with their own.

Anticipate criticism and respond to it. Professors are often quite impressed by an original and thoughtful defense to questions that have been posted before. Although Dr. Pagan may have already heard the defense of the faith that you offer, he or she may not be familiar with your treatment of the standard rebuttals to that defense. Think about how you would tackle the following loaded questions: "What evidence is there that Jesus was the Son of God?" "How can Christianity be worthy in light of the Crusades and the Inquisition?" "What about the sins of church leaders?"

Relax. You need not cover every aspect of biblical thought in every essay. Boldly do what the paper calls for and trust God for the results. Despite your best efforts to be direct yet sensitive, some readers will remain unpersuaded, even offended. This does not mean your project is a failure. In one respect, the worst that can happen is that you will learn something about composition, argumentation, human relations, the subject matter, or even about your faith. You are not responsible for converting your professor or for impressing your peers with your whizz-bang arguments. Instead of focusing solely on the outcome, try to see the assignment itself as an enriching experience.

When you do get overwhelmed by the task and your sense of responsibility, you might find some solace in the oft-forgotten fact that the bulk of Western (and some of Eastern) civilization is on your side. The Christian view, held by some of the brightest thinkers and compassionate activists in history, was predominant for centuries. Can we ignore this great host of humanity? The modern habit of dismissing Christianity with easy ridicule is usually evidence of conformist prejudice rather than the result of honest intellectual investigation.

Writer Dorothy L. Sayers encourages us to "drag out the divine drama from under the dreadful accumulation of slipshod thinking and trashy sentiment heaped upon it, and set it on an open stage to startle the world into some sort of vigorous reaction." Are you ready for a taste of intellectual derring-do? Certainly there are risks in challenging the status quo with the Christian perspective. But the rewards are great. Besides, what other options have integrity and offer such challenge? You wanted adventure, didn't you?

Field-Tested, Sensory-Satisfying Study Habits Guide

As I'm about to take this test,
I pray my brain will never rest.
But if it burns or fries or bakes,
That's one less test I'll have to take.

"How could I get a 'D'? I studied so hard for that exam!" Since teachers seem by nature heartless meanies you may be moaning that refrain before too long. My students invariably report that they put so many hours into studying for an exam that their poor grade must indicate some flaw in the system—namely, me. I agree in part with these disappointed students: There *is* a flaw in the system. And, while I'm open to discussing the possibility of unfairness in constructing or grading a given exam. I often discover that the problem is a glitch

221

called study habits. Intuition tells us that more hours should result in better marks, but if you are hitting a real nail with a toy hammer (or, worse yet, a peanut butter sandwich), hitting it harder or longer won't necessarily help. One good way to tool up for studying is the following system, a proven technique for hammering home knowledge without wasting energy or smashing your thumbs. I call it "The Sensual Approach."

Now, I know what you're thinking: "If I study in the hot tub, all the pages will get wet." I'll admit, "The Sensory Approach" is probably a more accurate term, but the first lesson in studying is getting your attention and keeping your concentration at a high level. You're with me so far, aren't you?

On with the Senses!

The "sensual" or "sensory" method of studying is developed from learning-theory research and assumes that retention is greatly enhanced through the use of as many senses as possible. Starkly put, what is more memorable—a spring rain that smells pungent, sounds pitter-pattery, feels wet, and looks drippy-droppery, or the description that you just read, which "touches" only your eyes? Although we have all read some wonderfully memorable sentences in our time, verbal impact is less complete than a fully sensory experience. So, based on the hope you are studying because of your desire to know truth and not merely to get a passing grade, I begin with the cry of much of the modern world: On with the senses!

Sight

Take those notes you've been studying for the upcoming exam. Since we all enjoy the obvious (that's why we listen when television news anchors talk with each other), I'll state this revolutionary tidbit: *Look* at your notes. No one else will do it for you. Stuffed under the pillow, shredded and eaten, burned during a prayer vigil, they are useless. These methods have been tested by thousands of college students in human-resource laboratories with the same results you have had: sleepless nights, upset stomachs, smoke-weary eyes, and rotten grades. Look you must.

But how to look? Look hard, look long, and look more than once. Underline the ideas that you think you need to remember, and do so as soon after the lecture as possible. (It will make things a lot easier if you do the underlining while the material is still fresh in your mind.) I can recall being faced with a comprehensive final exam and eighty pages of notes and wondering where to begin. It might take me several hours just to study them once! Although most students underline their texts as they read, they neglect to follow the same practice with their notes. *Engage your sight and underline your notes.*

Touch

Okay, now you have eighty pages of notes underlined. Big deal—it still takes light-years to read through them. The next hint is perhaps the most painstaking and therefore least-likely-to-be-followed suggestion: *Rewrite* the underlined portions onto another paper. You might think that you don't have the time for this, that you can't spare these hours "when you could be studying." First, this may be the best studying you can do. Second, your copied notes will save you from flipping laboriously and aimlessly through those eighty pages.

Not only are you making your notes more manageable, you are employing the sense of touch. Since your fingers are attached to the pen as you copy, you are "feeling" the written pattern of those facts and ideas. The rehearsal will come in handy on exam day. The same rewriting procedure should be done with your underlined texts. Copy the important points on a piece of paper. *Engage your touch and rewrite important information..*

Hearing

One other sense can be put into use effectively as you review your rewritten notes: Say them out loud and *listen*. In a secluded hideaway, whisper these not-so-sweet somethings in your ear. On a bus, in your car, on the plane, let your notes transport you as you hear them. Better yet, be dramatic! With panache, storm the Bastille of Biology with sound. With gestures in sync, deliver a fiery sermon about the characteristics of the Counter-Reformation. To this day I remember some of the particulars from a history exam because I paced from one room to another, shouting the answers to questions such as: "Was Abraham Lincoln a dictator during the Civil War?" And I only lost one roommate because of it!

You may feel foolish till you get the hang of it, but you'll feel more foolish with disappointing results on the old report card. *Engage your hearing and talk out your data.*

With no prejudice intended, I have neglected taste and smell. Personally, I'm rather fond of these senses, but I can't figure out a way to work them into this scheme. Unless a word technologist invents scratch-and-sniff notes, I'll probably never have to (oh, no, here it comes) eat my words.

The Extra Edges

If my experience as a student and teacher is any guide, you will notice measurable improvement by employing the sensory method. (If not, at least you'll find out who your real friends are.) Besides this approach, there are a few other practices that can also greatly increase your ability to understand and recall information.

The Organizational Edge

There is at least one snag in the sensory system. Despite good evidence to the contrary, it assumes that students begin with decent notes. Since you (or your friends) may need some help improving your note-taking, the following suggestions are provided. The first and rather parental point must be mentioned: Don't forget to brush, go to class, and pay attention. Besides that, as you take notes:

1. Divide your paper into three sections. On the left margin, doodle; on the right margin, whenever you can, make connections with other material in or out of the course, record any items to debate with your professors, and, especially, write out questions; in the center, summarize the essential ideas.

2. If in doubt of an item's importance, put it in your notes. You can't study what isn't on your paper.

3. Structure your notes so as to differentiate between major ideas and support for these ideas. I'm continually astounded by how rarely students use outlines. If you can't discern which are the main points and which are the subheadings, how can you expect your reader or exam-grader to do so? When your notes look like one long essay without paragraphs, you'll have a hard time figuring out what to underline. You could use standard outline technique or simply choose to vary your indentations.

The Psychological Edge

No, I'm not going to tell you to repeat the mantra: "I'm self-confidently smart. I'm self-confidently smart. I'm self-confidently smart." Instead, when copying your underlined notes, as reviewed in the section on "Touch," *condense* your work as much as possible. An entire course-load of notes can be put on one or two sheets of paper. You may think, "I can't read these itsy-bitsy words," but there is a great psychological advantage in being able to stare at one sheet of paper and realizing that this is what you need to know. Besides, how can you possibly be effective by reviewing eighty pages of notes, even if they are organized, underlined, and rewritten? The *Reader's Digest* method may destroy novels, but your notes are not meant to be a work of art.

The Creative Edge

Before you go blind from squinting at the tiny print you've entered on your study page, consider the inventive ways you can aid your memory and thus make your copied sheet more useful. One technique, which has been used ever since Greek schoolboys were trying to distinguish Plato from Playdoh, is image association. For raw memory work, such as foreign-vocabulary words or biological terms, imagining a picture from the word often helps trigger the meaning. For example, *archo* is the Koine Greek verb "to rule." You could memorize the meaning by imagining a giant king sitting on top of the Arch of Triumph.

Another creative memory aid is the use of acronyms. These are words formed by stringing together the initial letters of several other words. "MADD" means Mothers Against Drunk Drivers. When studying, make up an acronym that will represent what you need to remember. Suppose you need to know that Einstein was Smart, Time-conscious, Uranium-crazy, Pleasant, Irresponsible, and Dog-loving. Take the letters I've capitalized, put them together and you can say that Einstein was **STUPID**. Not only is this silly (and memorable on that ground alone), it also helps you to extract the six ideas from your notes.

The Energy Edge

Perhaps the most constructive, effective, common, and *ignored* advice about studying is to spread out your study times. So, I'll say it again: Except for the mnemonically gifted, cramming is the least effective way to study. Better to study fifteen minutes a day for two weeks than four hours the night before the test.

As in many of the other suggestions, the main issue here is self-discipline, not a lack of lack of knowledge about how to study. How can I encourage you to follow through on this? Maybe I could harass you with dorm food. The threat of "Surprise Loaf" could get *me* to do almost anything. Short of that, try dividing your study time into blocks for one term and see if you make any progress. As a freshman, I forced myself through several "all-nighters." As a graduate student, I was rarely hitting the books past eleven o'clock at night.

The Relational Edge

My last recommendation may change your life: Study with a friend (or friends). Although most students do this already, few have set up sufficient ground rules. Here are a few. First, each co-studier should come to the study session having completed *all* the above steps. Too often, students go to group sessions unprepared and leave with a false sense of confidence because of enlightening discussions. Unfortunately for these students, group knowledge will not be tested. Second, study partners should set up an agenda for the sessions: inventing acronyms and other image associations, drilling, question asking and answering, and so on. Without a plan, groups tend to get off the task. Third, groups should establish a suitably inspiring reward for studying well. A butter-pecan sundae or an afternoon at the pool will usually suffice. How will this change your life? You will at least get fat and tan. You may fall in love with someone while reviewing the relationship between rhetoric, dialectic, and poetic. You may also never see a "D" again.

In all, what I've suggested is simple. From your outlined, comprehensive, and underlined notes (Sight), condense your information (Touch), and create memory aids such as acronyms. In study time that you have divided into well-paced blocks, drill your material out loud (Hearing)—by yourself and with a friend. All that's left now is to begin. That's usually the hardest part. Maybe you should have a butter-pecan sundae just to get you started.

Recommended Reading

Introduction; Part One: You Can Take It with You

á Kempis, Thomas. *The Imitation of Christ*. London: Penguin, 1952.

Chesterton, G. K. *Orthodoxy*. Garden City, N.J.: Image Books, 1959.

Lewis, C. S. *Mere Christianity*. New York: Macmillan, 1964.

MacDonald, George. *Diary of an Old Soul*. Minneapolis: Augsburg Publishing House, 1975.

Malik, Charles. *The Two Tasks*. Westchester, Ill.: Cornerstone, 1980.

Wolterstorff, Nicholas. *Educating for Responsible Action*. Grand Rapids: William B. Eerdmans, 1980.

Part Two: The Angelic Beast in the Mirror

Buechner, Frederick. *Telling the Truth: The Gospel as Tragedy, Comedy, and Fairy Tale*. San Francisco: Harper & Row, 1977.

Kilpatrick, William Kirk. *Psychological Seduction*. New York: Thomas Nelson, 1983.

Packer, J. I. *Knowing God*. Downers Grove, Ill.: Inter-Varsity Press, 1973.

Pascal, Blaise. *Pensées*. London: Penguin, 1966.

Percy, Walker. *Lost in the Cosmos: The Last Self-Help Book You'll Ever Need*. New York: Washington Square Press, 1983.

Sayers, Dorothy L. *The Whimsical Christian*. New York: Macmillan, 1987.

Part Three: Those Whom We Love

Elliot, Elisabeth. *Passion and Purity*. Old Tappan, N.J.: Fleming H. Revell, 1984.

Lewis, C. S. *The Four Loves*. New York: Harcourt Brace Jovanovich, 1960.

Mason, Mike. *The Mystery of Marriage*. Portland, Ore.: Multnomah Press, 1985.

Trobisch, Walter. *I Married You*. San Francisco: Harper & Row, 1975.

White, John. *Eros Defiled*. Downers Grove, Ill.: InterVarsity Press, 1977.

Part Four: The Intellectual (!) Christian

Blamires, Harry. *The Christian Mind*. Ann Arbor: Servant Books, 1978.

Bloom, Allan. *The Closing of the American Mind*. New York: Simon & Schuster, 1987.

Gill, David. *The Opening of the Christian Mind*. Downers Grove, Ill.: InterVarsity Press, 1989.

Guinness, Os. *In Two Minds*. Downers Grove, Ill.: Inter-Varsity Press, 1976.

Muggeridge, Malcolm. *Christ and the Media*. Grand Rapids: William B. Eerdmans, 1977.

Pelikan, Jaroslav. "The Christian as an Intellectual." *Christian Scholar* 45 (1962): 6–11.

Sire, James. *The Discipleship of the Mind.* Downers Grove, Ill.: InterVarsity Press, 1990.

———. *The Universe Next Door.* Downers Grove, Ill.: InterVarsity Press, 1976.

White, John. *Flirting with the World: A Challenge to Loyalty.* Wheaton, Ill.: Harold Shaw, 1982.